The King Arthur Quest

Story Is About Research into
Whether King Arthur of Dark Ages Britain
Was a Real Historical Figure

Clayton Donoghue

THE KING ARTHUR QUEST
STORY IS ABOUT RESEARCH INTO WHETHER KING ARTHUR OF DARK AGES BRITAIN WAS A REAL HISTORICAL FIGURE

iUniverse books may be ordered through booksellers or by contacting:

iUniverse
1663 Liberty Drive
Bloomington, IN 47403
www.iuniverse.com
1-800-Authors (1-800-288-4677)

ISBN: 978-1-5320-5009-1 (sc)
ISBN: 978-1-5320-5010-7 (e)

Library of Congress Control Number: 2018909739

Print information available on the last page.

iUniverse rev. date: 10/03/2018

Contents

Acknowledgement

I 'd like to take this moment to acknowledge the assistance I have received from Lenisa Malfait and Nikkole Foley in putting this book together.

Introduction

The quest to know whether there really could have been a King Arthur.

*The funny thing about chasing the past, is that most people
wouldn't know what to do with it if they caught it.*
—Atticus Finch, *To Kill a Mockingbird*

Was Arthur actually a real king or simply a figment of
Geoffrey of Monmouth's wild imagination? King Arthur
is a colossal subject, and looking for a possible truth in it
all may seem an impossible task. Yet it is sheer curiosity to take a look
anyway. The one advantage I do have in this venture is despite the
enormous literature written on King Arthur, most of it is fictional.
The factual side of the man is not gigantic, and so the search here
is not that overwhelming. Where the King Arthur legend is centred
is primarily in south-east Wales. That quickly introduces the subject
of Celts, and believe it or not, it explains a lot. Celts are famous for
telling wild, exaggerated stories of their heroes—case in point, Finn
McCool of Ireland. The man was real; his accomplishments were
anything but. With that, I can quickly surmise King Arthur was likely
in the same realm. He was probably some local warrior who had an
exceptional gift for fighting, and of course the bards went crazy over
him. Today, we have this larger-than-life king with a magical sword
given to him by the Lady of the Lake. I guess calling it a quest sounds
a little fanciful for a hard-line history book, but in the light of the
subject, I think it fits rather well. If it turns out to be all surreal like
the Holy Grail was, then I can say it was indeed just a quest, and no
harm done.

I have a background in Celtic history, as well as one in mechanical
engineering. As such, two things are to my advantage. The first one

is I am familiar with Celts and how the bardic mind operates. This cuts down on a lot of time in research. Second, my engineering credentials allow me to know how correctly something goes together; and more important what parts are missing. I sense from the very beginning the Arthur story is more likely a case of missing parts than wild exaggeration, or a situation where the wheels on the car are far too small for the overpowering superstructure. Believe it or not, I have seen this kind of thing in the automotive industry, particularly with brakes and steering columns, where the material can't stand up to the forces of torque. Has King Arthur been burdened with too much fabrication so that the real man has been crushed by it all? My instincts say this is likely the case.

Because I have established that the real the King Arthur (if he was a king) was probably pretty insignificant, this automatically calls up the academic standard requirement. If I'm right and Arthur is nothing more than a Dark Ages warrior who was exploited by bards, then of course a substantial amount of proof is required, regardless of how trivial it turns out to be. Those of us who have been to university know there is a minimum prerequisite in documentation and literature needed, and I am certain I have met it in this quest. Whatever it turned up, the issue was my instincts were correct. It's not so much a search of verification as it is clearing away the rubble. As I went through the various research materials, I spent most of my time discarding evidence. Of course, this ends up being a tedious exercise for explaining why. Case in point, the most obvious example in the whole story about Arthur is he was put in the wrong century, according to the legend. Arthur is portrayed as a medieval knight in shining armour fighting the Anglo-Saxons. This is preposterous. There were no knights when the Saxons first came to Briton. The period Arthur lived in was known as the Dark Ages of the 5th century. That one observation encounters a score of explaining. And if you caught me using the word *Briton* instead of Britain, that too has to be explained. As it is, in the end, this book may feel like an exercise of pulling apart two squids that have their tentacles wrapped around each other.

One thing does need be mentioned in this book: there will be no trying to explain the unknown legends about King Arthur, like where is he buried and whether he is going to come back kind of stuff. In England and Wales, I am well aware that this is still a hot topic with such people like Allen Wilson. If King Arthur was in fact just a small-time warrior, then where he was buried hardly makes any difference as far as I'm concerned. Excalibur was just a myth, and so that too gets thrown out the window. Camelot is a different story. Here, I figured that has to be clarified. Where did Arthur actually live? Was it as grand as the stories say it was? After all, many of the grand Roman villas were in fact still standing and in good repair. As such, it is not inconceivable that he may have been living in one of these places, and it was called Camelot.

I did go through a lot of magazines as well as conventional textbooks, because I know they often will have the latest discoveries on the topic. As we know, archaeology is going on all the time. Unfortunately, here I discovered much of the material is mostly scams and sensationalism. A lot of them are looking for a fast buck to say they have the latest development on Arthur, but they have simply repackaged conventional research in bright colours. As it was, dismissing the popular literature was the easiest.

Regarding the mass media's interpretation of the Arthur legend, like many people, I have gone through a series of magazines where journalists claimed that they have been able to distinguish the true Arthur without even the slightest respectable measure of real research. While researching, I came across two magazines in this regard. I was shocked to see a major magazine publish such nonsense, and I wondered if they realise the backlash with their readers who are familiar with the subject. From this, I am only too aware to be careful that what is presented in this book will be from respectable sources. Throughout the book, I have openly referenced the sources where I got my material. I know this can be tedious and may at times compromise the storyline, but it was kept to a minimum so as not to be too tiresome. It was a delicate balancing act.

Now that you are aware of the parameters, it may be exciting. Then again, I am not going to mislead you: history is all about getting excited about removing old paint from your walls. It may not appeal to everyone, but I do know it improves once you start putting on a fresh coat, and suddenly the whole exercise is well worth going through. Note that there are a lot of people who paint over wallpaper and think it will stick, only to find that after a while, chunks start to peel off. I think this is what happened with King Arthur. Pieces are now falling off, and people are trying to paint over the holes when they should instead start fresh. I believe this book is one example of that line of thinking.

1

The Legend of King Arthur

King Arthur, half man, half myth,
Listen to the ground as it shifts,
A sword is locked in a stony grip,
Only the son of Briton will make it slip.

Then the call of Merlin to the great red dragon,
To breathe a fire upon the enemy Saxon.
They will burn on the shores of Kent,
Not knowing where to lament.

Vortigern too will smolder in the mountains of Powy,
His son who slashes at the serpent of Snowy,
Falls in the spray of the murky blood,
To vanquish the foe from where he stood.

Merlin waves his Rowan wand for Arthur to ride,
However the faeries of Avalon take him to hide.
Not sure if dead or alive reaches for the sordid chalice,
But it is only Percival who can avoid its total sollis.

—Donoghue

King Arthur looks down upon probably the most beautiful woman in all of Christendom. The shimmering blonde beauty is named Guinevere and, as Arthur pulls his horse around and leads his column of men out the fortress gate, she is not at a loss regarding his leaving. Once the heavy cavalry following Arthur are out of Camelot's walls, she quickly turns her eyes upon the handsome prince Sir Lancelot.

According to Norma Goodrich in her book *King Arthur,* the suspense between Guinevere and Lancelot is best told by the 12th-century author Chretien de Troyes. His story was openly and admittedly fictional, and yet in the romantic age of chivalry, many took the well-written version to be true. Such thinking gave him an even greater claim to fame when he introduced the subject of the Holy Grail. As we know, to this very day, this is by far the most captivating subject of the last thousand years. People like Dan Brown, in his book *The Da Vinci Code,* actually believe that the cup of Jesus's last supper truly exist. They couldn't be further from the truth, but it shows that our modern imagination is still as fertile as it was when Chretien first put pen to paper. This becomes the most important aspect to fully grasp as we begin to discover how it all began!

The three men who fully put the great "legend" of King Arthur together were Geoffrey of Monmouth, Chretien de Troyes and Sir Thomas Malory. What we see today out of Hollywood is the combined effort of these three men. From when Arthur first pulls Excalibur from the stone, to when the round table of knights was being formed, to Guinevere's affair with Lancelot and Arthur meeting his treacherous son Mordred at the fatal battle of Camlann—these were the doing of these three writers. The most interesting part of the opening stages of the Arthur legend is of course Geoffrey of Monmouth's version. He believed what he wrote was sincerely true British history. Based on the research material he had available at the time, it was not entirely unfounded.

Now that we have established where the complete story of Arthur originated from, the next crucial question is who amongst the three was the chief architect. The answer is none other than Geoffrey of Monmouth, in his book *Historia Regum Britanniae (The History of the Kings of Britain).* He lived in south-east Wales in the 1100s as a fairly high-ranking Celtic Welsh church official. I emphasize the word *Celtic* because we will soon discover just how important that word was to truly understanding the real King Arthur. Geoffrey lived in a time when Saxon Britain was going through what we would describe as a civil war between Empress Matilda and Steven of Blois. This war went on for close to a decade and resulted in a stalemate. When such turmoil is going on, you have to be very careful in what you say; it wouldn't take much to have your head cut off.

It is remarkable when we realise that even with the current politically sensitive environment Geoffrey was living in, he still went ahead and wrote *The History of the Kings of Britain*. In the title alone, it is clearly a story of a particular group of Britons who are certainly not Anglo-Saxon. In the 12th century, 80 percent of Briton was now under Anglo-Saxon control. Had the book not been as successful as it turned out to be, Geoffrey may have risked his very life writing it. It comes as no surprise that the Anglo-Saxons of "England" had very little use for the former Celtic Britons of Britannia. Anyway, Geoffrey, who is said to be a rather gifted writer, was hired by Walter, Archdeacon of Oxford, to write a conventional history book of the kings of Briton (Britain). To make a long story short, Geoffrey was supplied with a series of references from which to compose his own version of the British kings. The most notable reference he had was from a monk of the 9th century known as Nennius of Northumbria, who wrote a diatribe (history book) of Briton called *Historia Brittonum*. Though very difficult to read, the most incredible part of this book is the first mention of King Arthur in contemporary literature of the medieval period. Arthur's name had come before, but only on a local level, never on a national level like this. Nennius apparently does a very good job in describing King Arthur, because Geoffrey flies with the same king at the end of his book. As everyone knows in the academic world, Geoffrey used his very best artistic license skills to embellish Arthur as a hero of the Chivalric Age. In other words, Arthur, who was clearly of the Dark Ages Briton, was now a shining knight in armour from the 12th century. If you want to get an idea of just how shining King Arthur becomes, I strongly recommend you see the movie *Excalibur*, produced by John Boorman. King Arthur is so bright in his medieval armour that it is quite literally blinding. This King Arthur is nowhere near the King Arthur described by Nennius. Yet it did not matter—Geoffrey's knightly king was an instant sensation!

Again, in Norma Goodrich and Jean Markale's *The Celtic King*, we get a real feel for all the excitement that immediately followed the first publication of Geoffrey's *Historia*. No sooner did it reach the eyes of its first readers when another 230 copies were instantly "hand scribed." You have to realise there were no printing presses in those days, so if one wanted a copy of a book, it was handwritten. Think of the work that went into each book being made. As I understand it, there are still more than 20 copies of the original book still in existence. As a result, King Arthur swept the whole of Europe, and the fertile imagination of writers everywhere at once went into overdrive. Norma and Jean, as two sources alone, provide an overwhelming volume of medieval writers who start the first of the King Arthur legends. The most powerful name to come from hundreds of these authors is Chretien de Troyes.

Chretien de Troyes was a French writer who some say had his origins in Brittany. If true, we have our next "Celtic" writer expert in the ways of Bardic pros. He lived circa 1180 in the court of Marie of Champagne. Madame Marie was passionate about love stories, and she found that her Chretien was exceptional in captivating love adventures. No sooner did she come across Geoffrey's story of King Arthur that she employed Chretien to tell a fictional addition to it, but to make sure it was romantic! Chretien developed a hero we have all come to recognize as Sir Lancelot. He then went on to transform a real Guinevere from Scotland (AD 575) to have a love affair with the handsome knight. The great twist in the story is that of course she was to be the wife of King Arthur. With the one move, we have set the stage for a classic Shakespearean love tragedy. And to truly make things interesting, Chretien adds in the villainous character Mordred. Further, this is no ordinary villain. Mordred is the son of an incestuous affair Arthur had with his sister Morgause (Morgana). Norma Goodrich claims that Chretien had enormous difficulty putting this juicy rendition together, and officially the story was never fully finished. However, whatever stage he stopped at it was more than enough for Marie. She at once wanted copies of this version to share with all her friends, and before long it was accepted as an official version to the original story by Geoffrey. Of course, the story does not end there. Chretien goes on to develop his masterpiece and that is the famed Holy Grail.

The Holy Grail invention had its origins from the crusade that was now well underway. Once the crusaders had taken Jerusalem, people claimed they were finding antiquities of Jesus. One of the big sensational finds was the actual nails that were used to his crucifixion. It was at this time that the cross of Jesus was said to be in Constantinople, found by an expedition by Queen Helena of Constantine the Great. All of it was pure nonsense, but the superstitious imagination of the times was uncontrollable. Chretien added the most inspiring subject of all, and that was Jesus's chalice. Though complete fabrication, it swept like a grass fire across the whole of the continent. Soon countries like Greece and Spain came out saying the Holy Grail (the Chalice) was in fact true, and they had the actual cup. You can visit these countries today and see for yourself; they still have these cups enshrined, verifying their claims.

The legendary story wouldn't be complete unless we make mention of the famous Percival and the great battle of Camlann by none other than Sir Thomas Malory. Thomas is our last great writer who finishes our Hollywood version of Arthur with his famous book *Le Morte d'Arthur (The Death of Arthur)* in 1415. What's interesting about Malory's addition is it may have been all forgery. It has been recently found that another book with the exact same title was written two hundred years earlier. Whatever the truth, it doesn't matter. What counts is that Malory's version is what sold. In the age of the great printing press (1400s), for the first time the story of King Arthur was mass produced in the thousands, and Malory became another sensation. For a second time, King Arthur screams across not only the whole of Europe but now the new world as well. However, it must be remembered that the Thomas Malory sequel is just another fictional story. From this latest excitement, King Arthur is officially carved in stone.

If you are a little confused, I completely understand. I fully implied that King Arthur was a real person in my introduction, and now in the very first chapter, it's pretty obvious he was completely fictional. This is where the story becomes interesting. The clue to knowing whether there is any legitimacy to a real King Arthur involves going back to Geoffrey of Monmouth. As we now know, he discovered King Arthur from the monk Nennius. Nennius was completely convinced Arthur was real, and so Geoffrey went with this as well. He wrote him up like everyone else did in his *Historia*, no bigger, no smaller. Arthur only became a significant subject because of one major event, and that was the Battle of Badon. Nennius found that the name Arthur was frequently used in Welsh records like the *Annals of Cambriae,* and so he did not question it. The name was in numerous situations associated to the famed battle, and so Nennius simply accepted it as fact.

With the Battle of Badon, we have an all new King Arthur. Here we are forced to rip ourselves away from Geoffrey's creative embellishments of the 12th century and crawl our way back to the brutal world of the Dark Ages. When we go down this road, the medieval King Arthur, who as we know is near 100 percent fictional, suddenly has evidence of actually being true. The key to the second story is putting King Arthur where he originated from. Right up to King Charles II of England, Arthur was in fact believed to be true. The problem was the Geoffrey version was what everybody was basing their arguments on. I like how archaeologist and historian Francis Pryor, of *Making of the British Landscape,* put it: "the whole thing was complete rubbish." The Geoffrey version of Arthur had very little substance to do with the real King Arthur. It was because of him that the "Legendary Arthur" was born. And because Wales, from which the real Arthur likely came, was of very little importance to the Norman and Anglo aristocrats, no one was interested in checking the real records. It didn't occur to anyone at the time that there were no knights in shining armour when the Saxons first landed on the shores of Kent around AD 435.

With that, you must feel the rug has been pulled out from your feet, because the legendary Arthur is what nearly everybody knows. How is it that there is another Arthur, and this time he may be actually real? Further, the most important question is, Is he the same person? The answer is yes and no. King Arthur is the same person in reality as he is in the legends. What happens is Geoffrey of Monmouth takes the (5th century) Dark Ages king with most of his followers and places him in a 12th-century fictional world. The real King Arthur ran around in chain mail and wolfskins. Geoffrey found that King Arthur would never do in medieval England, and so he glams him up a bit with shimmering armour and a beautiful castle he called Camelot. For the most part, the story is accurate but a little confusing. How did people like the Saxon warlord Hengist of the 5th century suddenly appear in a 12th-century world? Well, it didn't matter, and nobody cared. All people wanted was to read how the fictitious love story between Sir Lancelot and Guinevere ended, even if the historical facts didn't make sense.

Now that we have been jarred and twisted into knowing there is a real King Arthur; where is this starting point? Nennius, a Welsh monk of the 9th century, is where we begin, and from there we travel backward. Nennius wrote a book called *Historia Brittorium*. Most of the material in the Rebook was based on the writings of two previous Briton monks. The first one was Gildas the Wise of the 5th century, and the second one was Bede the Venerable of the 9th century. Gildas, who wrote *De Excidio et Conquestu Brittaniae*, is the crucial figure to the real King Arthur, for he actually lived in Arthur's time. Gildas was born in AD 500 and died in AD 570. The real Arthur is accepted by most scholars as having been born circa AD 478 and died in AD 539. These dates will be verified as this book progresses. For now, it is enough to know Gildas was a young man when the real King Arthur was fighting off the enemies of "Camelot." Bede, who wrote *Historia Ecclesiastica Gentis Anglorum,* where much of the Dark Age Period material came from, used Gildas. Technically, Gildas is the one we should start with, but it is Nennius who starts the ball rolling by claiming it was King Arthur who fought at the famous battle. Gildas and Bede mention Badon, but they do not mention Arthur. In this one move, Gildas and Bede are made superfluous. Along with this, Nennius is also the first to do a little bit of embellishment on Arthur, and later Geoffrey goes crazy with it. It is because of Nennius's fantastic literary creativity that Geoffrey ends up getting the primary focus for much of what is written on Arthur.

The main events that the three monks centred on the real Arthur's activities were the Picts and the Irish raids and the Anglo Saxon invasion. From what was written on this, it was not hard to date the period to the 5th century. When the Romans left Britannia (as it was called then) in AD 410, these three barbaric groups swarmed the island. There were no gallant knights in those days, and Gildas makes that perfectly clear, as does Bede. If you saw the movie *King Arthur* from 2004 starring Clive Owen and Keira Knightley, the dress, especially the Saxons', is probably the best example of what the world looked like at this time. The Saxons wore animal skins, and the Celtic Britons wore tartans and covered their bodies in blue tattoos. Hadrian's Wall, which stretched for miles, was now an empty ghost town. The doors were wide open, and the Picts were now freely coming and going. They had a huge army, as Tacitus claimed, and wasted no time pillaging the East Coast of Britannia, going as far south as Londinium (London) itself. They were under the command of the war genius Drest of a Hundred Battles. His activities were well recorded in the *Pictish Chronicles*. On the West Coast, more than 200 ships were seen regularly commanded by the wild Irish pirate-king known as Niall of the Nine Hostages. He was taking Roman Britons as slaves by the thousands, according to Saint Patrick. Last but hardly least are the Saxons, under the command of the infamous Hengis. He was given the Island of Thanet by Vortigern, just south of Londinium, but because he was impatient, he took all of the modern county of Kent. Smelly wolfskins, tartan wools and bloody axes were the most common apparel seen at this time. The classy, clean, white Roman toga had long-since disappeared.

"Typical Dark Age Royal Court"

For the next hundred years, the returned Celtic Briton is in a see-saw war (primarily with the Saxons), and things looked pretty bleak. The reason I say returned to *Celtic Briton* is because this was what the country was before the Romans came. After they left, they returned to their previous cultures on account that the Romans did not occupy Briton in the same manner as they had the rest of the empire. This will be explained in more detail in the next two chapters.

Getting back to the brutal Saxons, according to Gildas, Bede and finally Nennius, a miracle happens in AD 515 at Badon. Badon is where the Britons defeated the Saxons, and from it everything comes to an abrupt stop. The Anglo-Saxon invasion basically stops right in the middle of Briton. Archaeologists have confirmed that for the next 25 years, there is peace across the land. Francis Pryor, author of *Briton AD,* fully acknowledges the only name that they have on record who was likely responsible for this unexplained phenomenon is a man named Arthur, famously known as King Arthur. He accepts Nennius's claim that it was Arthur who fought and won the Battle of Badon. If there was another man who had won this other than Arthur, historians have yet to reveal his identity.

2

The Celts

> Physically the Celts are a terrifying in appearance, with deep sounding and very harsh voices. In conversation they use few words and speak in riddles, for the most part hinting at things and leaving a great deal to be understood. They frequently exaggerate with the aim of extolling themselves and diminishing the status of others. They are boasters and threateners and given to bombastic self-dramatization, and yet they are quick mind and with good naturalability for learning.
>
> —Diodorus Siculus

The word *Celt* was mentioned in just about every book I read on King Arthur. Except for Jean Markale, none of the authors took the time to explain the significance the Celtic heritage had in the Arthurian legend. I discovered it is very important, and an effort should have been made to show the role it had in the overall picture. I suppose because Geoffrey put Arthur in the medieval setting, the Celtic aspect was lost. Now that we have Arthur in the correct time frame, the Dark Ages, the Celtic element becomes a relevant subject to exam.

To start things off, the name Arthur is a Deisi Celt name. The Deisi Celts came to south-west Wales circa AD 260 from southern Ireland. They formed a small community in the Celtic nation known as Demetae. The Deisi, like all Celtic tribal nations, had their own identity for a number of subjects, and the name Arthur was one of them. Knowing this one aspect in the very beginning helps to not only identify Arthur but also find the likely location of where he came from.

Demetae continues to be an independent Celtic Briton nation up until AD 375, when the Irish Ard-Ri (High King) King Eochaid takes it over. It remains under Irish control for the next 300 years. This is well past the time when King Arthur was the king of Briton. Culturally speaking, the Irish had an influence on the surrounding areas for a considerable period of time. If this was the case, the first natural question is, Was King Arthur Irish, and did he come from Demetae (later to be Dyfed)? It turns out the answer is no to both questions. The royal pedigrees of Demetae do not have a King Arthur in the century, but there is an Arthur dated to the late 6th century. Unfortunately, this is not the Arthur we are looking for.

However, because the name is Celtic, and most historians do have an Arthur in Wales or south-west Briton, then of course the Celtic heritage should be examined to at least see what relevance it may play in the whole story.

Prior to the Romans arriving under Emperor Claudius circa AD 43, Briton was a Celtic nation in the purest form of the definition. Most of Briton was not really conquered but was in a client state status. When the Romans left, the island returned to its Celtic infrastructure. Therefore the Celtic subject is a relevant consideration.

Celts were a people who occupied virtually the whole of Europe from 350 BC to 55 BC, when the Romans started making serious inroads on their territories. They did not evolve as a society to the same level of sophistication as the Greeks, Romans and Egyptians, and so they are often denigrated to the identity of being simply an Iron Age subculture. To the Romans, the Celts were regarded with even a cruder status of primitive barbarians. Yet it is strange that on many levels, the Celts were more advanced than the Romans were, especially in metallurgy, the arts and democracy.

Way up in the mountains of Austria, closest to the Swiss border, is a place called Halstatt. It was here in 800 BC that 3 major cultural groups converged: the Scythians, the Germans and the Dorics. From 800 to 350 BC, this combined group of people were the first identified by the Greeks as Keltoe, later to be changed to Kelts (Celts). There was a major evolutionary change with these people starting in 350

BC. Their modern identity was to come from their place of origin, the Halstatt Celts.

The Halstatt Celts were a society with much the same political and social infrastructure as anything one would see in the ancient Mediterranean world, but at a less developed evolution. On an economic level, they were the biggest supplier of salt in the known world. Today, you can still visit their enormous salt mines. In return, the Keltoes imported gold and wine primarily from the Etruscans and Greeks. In south-west Germany, closest to the Austrian border, in 1977 the famous Hochdorf Royal burial site was discovered. The site was remarkably well-preserved and from the Halstatt Age. The site is dated to 350 BC, and it by many claimed to represent the height of the Halstatt Celt culture. Here, it was found that individual artefacts of the three original groups, plus Greek and Etruscan, were present. The Halstatt Celts were still not a homogenous culture.

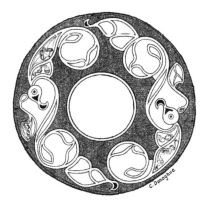

"Hallstatt Celtic Design"

The degree of riches found in the Hochdorf clearly explained why in 350 BC there was a mass migration that spread across Western Europe and reached as far as Portugal and Ireland. They had grown in both size and wealth so that they could no longer be confined to the borders of Austria. The Halstatt culture did evolve to the extent that they created their own language; we know it today as Goedelic Gaelic. It is primarily from their language that historians were able to track the expanse of their migration.

Then starting in 350–250 BC, the Celts of Austria went through another major cultural evolution. In their migration, they moved their capital from Halstatt to a place now known as La Tene, Switzerland. Here, a whole new Celtic culture developed. Like before, a burial site of a thousand graves in La Tene was discovered at the turn of the 20th century. The art form of these Celts was very distinct, with no outside influences to the design. The art form became their distinguishing identity. It was resolved that the Celts as a culture had at last fully come onto their own. It comes as no surprise that from the discovery, the Celts of this location were named La Tene Celts. Thus, we have pre-350 BC Halstatt Celts and post-250 BC La Tene Celts.

In 250 BC, the Celts are once again overpopulated, and another major migration takes place, but on a much larger scale. They not only migrated to most of Western Europe as far as Britain, but they also stretched themselves into Italy, Yugoslavia, Greece and Northern Turkey. This group of Celts also had their own distinct language, which from the research in Britain today is known as Brithonic Gaelic. The style of language is still very much in use on the western fringes of Wales. Language experts are able to define the furthest reaches of the Halstatt and La Tene Celts throughout the UK and Ireland strictly based off the two languages still in use.

The Celtic Empire
400 BC - 50 BC

Halstatt

La Tene

WWW.FREEWORLDMAPS.NET

What has to be mentioned at this point is another civilization that predates the arrival of the Celts: the Urnfield people. This name is a result of the type of pottery they made. The Urnfield civilization had occupied Western Europe from about 2500 BC right up till 350 BC. This culture didn't fully disappear upon the arrival of the Celts. The Urnfield people had a major cultural influence on the Celts that arrived in Scotland, and religiously speaking with the Celts that came into France and England. This point will become important later on in the understanding of the Celts and the Druids.

It is now understood that the British Isles were subject to two major migrations of Celts (Halstatt and La Tene). Further, except for Scotland, the Celts became the dominant culture of Britain and Ireland. From here, we now move to understand who the Celts were and how they impacted the age of King Arthur.

From the Germanic and Scythian elements, Celts in general were a warlike people, highly skilled in the use of a sword and brilliant horsemen. Horse-riding evolved into charioting; the art form may have been picked up from the Hittites. From their Doric influence, they were a very ingenious people, particularly in metallurgy, and this distinct craftsmanship became fully developed in AD 500. Celtic metal was a mixture of tin, copper and iron. The metal was folded much in the same manner of a Japanese samurai sword. As it a result, it was a very durable and high-quality steel that not even the Romans were capable of replicating.

Celtic society is admittedly much more primitive than the Romans and Greeks. They did not live in cities like Rome or in rectangular homes with oil lamps. Celts lived in small, round, thatched-roof cottages that barely fit one small family. They did not have furniture as we understand it; they ate and slept on a wolfskin-covered ground. These small cottages were often grouped into small wooden palisade fortresses known as raths, or if on water, crannogs. About five or six families would make up a rath. Sanitation was pretty rough, and combined with the warrior-like mentality of the men, the average life expectancy was around 30 years at best.

A series of raths developed into what was known as a clan, or Tùath chiefdoms. The number could vary from a dozen to well more than 100, as was found in the case of France and Scotland. The next level up was a provincial Tùath kingdom. Ireland had the best example of this with Munster, Leinster, Connaught and Ulster all being forms of royal provincial Tùath. Finally, there was the overall kingdom, such as was the case of Ireland and Scotland. In Ireland, the capital was in Tara, and in north-east Scotland it was in Inverness. The kings who were elected were referred to as an Ard-Ri, in Gaelic meaning High King. Also, at the rath and provincial Tùath level, the leaders were elected as petty kings. More on the political infrastructure will be explained later. Celtic Briton had a similar political setup as in Ireland and Scotland. It is unconfirmed, but it is felt Castle Maiden or Cadbury Castle, from their enormous sizes, may have been the location of their Ard-Ri. If we are to use Vortigern as an example, the Britons were certainly familiar with the system after the Romans left. Viriconium (Wroxeter, England) became their Ard-Ri centre in the 5th century, but it later believed moved to Cadbury.

There is a description by the Greek writer Strabo of what the Celts looked like when they arrived in Delphi in 350 BC. Many wore a conical steel helmet with horns or an animal motif on the top. They wore brightly coloured woollen shirts and plaid design pants called trews. Across their shoulders was again a plaid-designed cape fastened at one side with a huge brooch. Finally, nearly every Celt carried a longsword or spear. Again, the quality of these weapons was the closest semblance of actual steel, because the Celts were the best at making weapons in the whole of Europe. For the most part, the men were clean-shaven except for a massive Manchu-like moustache. The colour of hair was blond, and the average height was 5' 10." They were giants compared to the Romans, whose average height was 5' 5."

"Typical Celtic Warrior"

The Celts were extremely competent horsemen and had the best-designed chariots for the rough terrain of Briton. The reason for this is because the platform from which the warrior stood on was suspended by a rope frame, not on the axle, as was the case with Egyptian chariots. It made for a much more comfortable ride and was a stable platform from which the warrior could throw his spears.

As Julius Caesar testified in *Commentarii de Bello Gallico*, the Celts were not a very well-structured society. He recognized a problem in their elected leadership system. Often decisions were based on a group consensus. As it was, they could not make timely decisions with any degree of coordination. The Battle of Alesia, where Vercingetorix went up against Caesar in 52 BC, was probably the most tragic example of a decentralized command structure. Because Vercingetorix was an elected leader, he was compelled to request assistance against the Romans rather than order it, as a general would do. It cost him the battle on account of unnecessary delays. This will be a serious issue to recognize in Briton with King Arthur, because many say he was not so much a king as he was a Dux Bellorum (Duke of Battle). In his 12 battle campaigns leading up to Badon, he was compelled to drag along with him the other kings of the Welsh confederacy. It was the agreement he was forced into if he was going to have any troops for his army, clearly exposing a typical Celtic political infrastructure not suffered in the Saxon ranks as well. The campaign went on for about 10 years or more, and so it is likely much of it was due to internal discussion of all the various chiefs. Nennius says Arthur was successful in all of his battles, which would indicate Arthur was a much more persuasive leader than Vercingetorix.

The internal affairs of Celtic society were unique as a result of its style of leadership. As we know, at the very top is an elected king. He was elected by a combination of his peers and the shaman group known as Druids. Above them came the Arch Druid. He was, as Caesar correctly identified, a very powerful figure. The king could not make a decision on any serious issue without first consulting with the Arch Druid first. After the Druids came the warrior captains and provincial Tuath kings. In Ireland, they were easily definable, representing Connaught, Leinster, Ulster, and Munster. In Briton, they would have represented Powy, Glywysing, Dumnonia, Gwynedd and Demetae. However, remember that the Britons did not have a permanent Ard-Ri, so to speak. There was a more fluid hierarchy system.

Then came the Brehons and the artisans. Brehons were a kind of a mobile legal system wrapped into one person. If there was a dispute, a Brehon would come to your house and, by the authority of the king, resolve any legal issues in a given community. Artisans included both musicians (known as bards) and jewellers. They were a highly prized group that could travel the country freely, applying their trade. Everyone knew not to abuse them in any form because they had special protection from all the provincial kings. After them were the farmers, smiths and freemen. What made them important to the kingdom was that they could own land; to the king, they represented his tax base. They were definitely protected under Brehon law. The lowest level was the slaves. However, it has to be noted that Celtic slaves were generally treated much better than Roman slaves. The reason was that slaves were generally more expensive in comparison to Roman slaves. A Celtic slave usually cost the price of three pigs, and three pigs added up to the price of one cow. A cow was the most expensive commodity in the Celtic economy. When you consider that an average rath only had 4 or 5 cows on it, owning a slave was serious decision. Thus Celts were careful about how they treated their slaves. In the book of Ulster, it was reported that when St, Patrick was a slave, he was allowed to attend the annual Samhain festival with a limited degree of freedom. There is a bit of a verification on how slaves were treated in the British Isles.

Let's move on to Druids. We have heard so much about them, and of course Merlyn is fully identified as being one. This mysterious group of shamans were a central characteristic of the Arthur legend. Therefore, understanding what Druids are is vitally important.

Many historians feel strongly that Druids originated from the Urnfield people. Once more, the Urnfield people were in Briton prior to the arrival of the Celts. They are the ones who built Stonehenge, and most of the stone circles and passage graves are also credited to them. Clearly it was a much more sophisticated society than is commonly known. They assimilated themselves to the Celts when they arrived in Gaul (France), Hybernia (Ireland), Iberia (Spain) and Britannia. The Druid had very mysterious witchcraft skills, and so it was initially hard for them to move up the rank structure of the superstitious Celtic world. However, because they were a well-educated group, they soon figured around the superstition and worked their way into the Celtic political structure, where they eventually dominated.

It took 20 years to train a person to become a full Druid. High ranking Druids were commonly recognized with the wearing of white robes. In the training stages leading up to a high Druid, there were several levels of official accomplishment stages. The stages were represented first as bards, next as Brehons, then royal pedigree historians and finally High Druid. The lower-ranking Druids had coloured robes from which distinguished the various groups. From a modern Welsh Druid website, unofficially, it looked like the rank structure was black, blue, green and finally white. Given that the number of colours lines up with the number of positions, it stands to reason this may be the colour scheme they actually used.

A Druid's training involved the study of astrology, history, botany, poetry, medicine, genealogy, pagan religion, rhetoric and Ogham communication. It was a very complex and in-depth education system. The most fascinating aspect to all of this is that there was no written language—everything was memorized. The way things were memorized was through their poetry, and thus we have the famous oral tradition standard. The poems were named bards, after the title of bard. It is a small point but is something to be aware of when people are saying a bard, meaning a Celtic poem. Also, bards were generally difficult in nature: a minimum-sized bardic poem consisted of nine stanzas of three-line rhyming sentences. The minimum standard to be certified as a Bard is to know 31 bards. The longest known bard of the Celtic world is called the Y-Gododdin, composed by Aneirin (recognized as a Brythonic Bard). It is said the bard had close to a hundred stanzas in it. In the time of Brian Boru (AD 1100) Ireland he was claimed to know 100 bards—and he was a king, not a Bard. My apologies if this is beginning to sound a little tedious. It does give you an idea of just how much training is required to simply be a Bard or Druid. Now, imagine if the Bard wants to go on and become a Brehon. He now has to learn the law, which entails another series of statute bards. It is scary to think the degree of mind discipline that was required to qualify as a full Druid.

Here is an example of a typical bardic poem. The date is officially unknown but is claimed to be 3rd[th] century Irish via oral tradition.

Chε Gaε Bulg

I am the stone that lies beneath the ground
I am the trees that cover the mountain high
I am the fire that burns the stone
I am the ore that merges with the ash
I am the heat that makes the steel
I am the steel that creates the sword
I am the Morgan who covets the sword
I am Cu chulain flying in my chariot
I am death that sings through the Duir of Connaught

—Ulster Bard, third century

The bardic poem is where most of King Arthur's legend has come down to us. There is an addition to the straight poetic bard, and that is the bardic stories. They are of course much longer and are not written in bardic stanzas, yet they do follow a bardic fantasy principle. The greatest example of this is the famous "Mabinagion." It is a collection of Dark Ages Welsh stories, chiefly of King Arthur, compiled by a Lady Grey in the 19th century. The objective is not to record history directly but to come up with a factious story in order to glorify or demean a person and, in some very small way, reflect a real event or tragedy. For example, the story of the quest for the Holy Grail is a well-known example of this type of writing. Though it was written in the 12th century, it did follow the Celtic fantasy guidelines. The idea here is to have a creative enough story that will be remembered. The more outrageous it is, the better the chance it will survive the test of time. The quest for the Hole Grail definitely falls into this category. It is completely untrue but was so well-written by Chretien de Troyes that to this very day, it is the most remembered stories of all the King Arthur legends.

Experts date and categorise the bards and bardic stories based on how they were written or recorded. For example, in the poem "Consolation," what dates it is the word *goidelic*. It was not a term used in the Dark Ages. Bede is one of our best measuring sticks in this regard, because he knew the Irish and Welsh were both Celtic but spoke different languages (Goidelic and Brythonic). He was unfamiliar with the two cultures of Halstatt and La Tene, and so he simply says the two groups spoke Irish and Welsh. His timeline was in the 8th century. Therefore, the poem had to been written sometime after the 8th century. Obviously, the person who wrote this poem was sophisticated enough that he was familiar with the two types of Celts. The earliest language distinction of Goidelic and Brythonic by scholar's dates to the 10th century. Thus, it is likely "Consolation" was written in that century. It's with this type of sophistication that modern scholars are able to pinpoint whether certain bards were of oral tradition or were more contemporary.

This shows how historians like Jean Markle can precisely tell whether it is a bard or a bardic story, and when it was likely first told. As we now know, there is a format that they have to follow. What I have found going through this part of the King Arthur story is how amateurs who know absolutely nothing of the Celtic culture are well-justified in giving an opinion on it. I find this particular type of behaviour common practice with mostly British and American historians. A typical amateur distortion is they read something at face value and quickly express an uninformed observation on it. The classic example of this is the numerous medieval events, such as the sword being pulled from the stone, the primary source coming from Geoffrey of Monmouth. The contemporary historian sees this and is too quick to say that could not have happened. On the surface he is right, but that is not the whole story, and simply because he or she is too lazy to dig deeper, we are stuck with this poorly researched statement. Hopefully now that we have a better idea to the background culture of King Arthur, this kind of nonsense can be identified and quickly disregarded.

It seems the above-mentioned problem has its source in the proper identity of the Celts. Many European historical sources prefer to call the Celts "Iron Age people." I know in Great Britain, Spain and Denmark, this is a very prevalent point. My visit to the National Museum of Copenhagen provided probably the best explanation as to why the Iron Age term is more acceptable. They argue that because the Celts chiefly operated on a local level, their culture is not fully universal from Galatia to Iberia and up to Caledonia, regardless of the fact that they all speak the same language, wear similar clothes, enjoy the same types of art, and had universal politics across the continent. From what I can tell, because the Celts did not have a central government like Rome, they were merely a patchwork of different tribes. In this sense, you can't call them a homogeneous society.

The problem with this type of thinking is that it allows for distortion and misrepresentation, which is clearly the case here. For example, openers on this argument are that Iron Age people don't have a culture. As it is, there are no rules to follows in behaviour. If you include all the Iron Age societies throughout the Mediterranean world, you have an explosion of different cultures—Roman, Greek, Etruscan, Egyptian, Persian, Hittite, German and Celtic. It's a fact that they all had distinct borders to the types of cultures that lay inside them. How you can recognize the problem is simply by saying Rome was also an Iron Age society. The moment you say that, you quickly realise this is wrong. You cannot put Romans in the same camp with Celts, even though categorically it is accurate. Americans and Canadians are both North Americans. In the United States, this not so much an issue as it is in Canada. Though it is completely accurate, Canadians know the abbreviation to the term is American, and that would put them as US Americans, which is completely unacceptable. Therefore, the term "Iron Age people" is an inappropriate, generic simplification of the specific culture of Celts.

What is amusing on all this is the term "Iron Age people" is never used when it comes to King Arthur, but only the term Celt. Therefore, it is one more reason why the "Iron Age" term has to be eliminated, and the reference of Celt has to be firmly applied. If there are no Celts, then half the books written on Arthur don't make any sense, because they keep referring to a background culture that doesn't exist. Therefore, in order to keep some sense of continuity on the Arthur story, you are forced to say that the Celts were a genuine, distinct society, just as Quebec is to Canada. Now, if that doesn't turn heads, I don't know what will.

3

Briton before and during Rome

Before Rome

The time is circa 55 BC. Julius Caesar has just finish putting down the rebellions in Gaul, and now he is amassing an army to go over to the island a Roman consul, Brutus, has named

Briton. Caesar is hoping to recruit some members of the Atrebates Celts to come along with him, but nobody is interested in the idea. The reason he wants to bring some of them along with him is to use them as interpreters, as well as proof he comes in peace.

On the other side of the modern English Channel, just west of Kent, is an area occupied by Briton Atrebates. They have made known they will welcome the Romans when they come. It turns out it was true. The Briton Atrebates allowed the Roman ships to land and the army to come ashore. However, that is as far as the welcome committee went. Once the Romans move inland, they are immediately attacked by the neighbouring Belgae, Cantii and Trinovante Briton Celts. Everything quickly turns into a fiasco, and Caesar is forced to withdraw.

The following year, Caesar tries again to invade the Briton Celts, and again he fails. As we know, he never comes back. It isn't until AD 43 that Emperor Claudius orders Aulus Plautius to invade the Island. This time the Romans are successful in getting a permanent foothold, and thus begins a siege of the Britons for the next 50-odd years. Under Agricola in AD 71, the Romans push their way as far as the borders of Scotland. In those days, Scotland was known as the land of the Picts. Scotland as we know it does not come into existence until AD 700. The Picts were a combination of Halstatt Celt and Urnfield people. Scholars examining the Pictish language have found both uniquely (allege) Urnfield and Goidelic words in it. Thus, as Bede put it, they spoke Pictish.

For the next 300 years, Rome has as much difficulty holding onto Briton as it did with Iberia (Spain). Rebellions seem to come almost every 50 years, and in the late 4th century, Rome had enough of the barbarians and started packing up to leave. By AD 410, they were completely gone. On its own again, Briton returned to its former self almost overnight. Close to 400 years of Roman domination had virtually no effect on the island people. The Romans made a mistake in their occupation of the Britons in that they did not assimilate the Celts into fully being Romans, as they did with the Celtic Gauls. In Briton, the Roman culture only stretched to the borders of Wales, Dumnonii and Hadrian's Wall. In these three parts of the country, the Romans simply built garrisons next to the Celtic fortresses such as Cadbury Hill fortress and Maiden Castle. The Britons were allowed to carry on as they did before. What you saw in Briton, unlike in Gaul, was the local traditional tartan dress walking alongside the Roman toga. As it was, you had two distinct societies cohabiting. Thus when the Romans left, the Celtic forts were still in operation, and the locals were able to re-establish their former kingdoms. For example, Silures (Glywysing), Ordovice, Dumnonii, Brigantes (Rheged) and Demetae all re-emerged.

The following is a bit of a repeat of the Celt chapter, but it's on the local level.

In about 350 BC, the Urnfield Briton witnessed the first onslaught of Halstatt Celts. If it wasn't made clear before, the Celts were vicious in nature. Though historians like to sanitise their appearance in Briton as a migration, the truth is it was more of a conquest. The Urnfield culture was all but wiped out except in Scotland. The only thing that remains of the Urnfield people is their famous standing stones (Stonehenge). Here again, another oddity takes place, and that is many of the artistic traits of the Urnfield people are incorporated into Celtic art. The Trident symbol, for example, was clearly an Urnfield art form that was passed on to the Celts. It is because of this that many uninformed historians have taken the position that the Urnfield people were simply an early form of Celts, which isn't true at all. What you have to do is take a moment and examine the La Tène art form, comparing it with Urnfield; then you will quickly see the difference. The triangular design is strictly a Urnfield concept. The La Tène design is strictly in a straight-line application with when using their circles

Then in 250 BC, it happens all again. This time, invaders are La Tène Celts. They sweep to the Irish Sea border of Wales and Cornwall and to the southern border of Scotland, but they go no further. Ireland and Scotland are not touched. The Gaelic language in its two forms are evidence to knowing precisely where the two invasions reached. Based on archaeological evidence, the second invasion was just as fierce as the first one. The Halstatt Celts were fully assimilated into the La Tène Celts. Basically, all traces of the Urnfield culture was completely gone, and Briton was now thoroughly Celtic. We know the Celts in general are a fierce, determined people by nature, and so it is not hard to understand that when the Romans leave, they are only too happy to go back to the way they were. From Francis Pryor's research, it was as if overnight, the Roman villas and civitas were completely abandoned. The Roman togas were quickly discarded for the old woollen trews. Archaeological evidence shows that the Britons looked very much in AD 411 as they did in AD 33.

The Briton Celts returned to their small raths, and after the AD 405 civil war, they removed all traces of their former Roman political infrastructures. Taxes were once more back on the barter system. Roman coins were replaced with livestock as the main form of currency. The provincial kingdoms like Silures and Demetae once again have the real authority, and the national leader, the Ard-Ri (High King), acts more like a president.

Having said that, one thing has to be mentioned. Those who know their British history are fully aware the person who comes to power at this time (AD 420) is Vortigern. He was anything but a president when compared to the Ard-Ri of Ireland. Vortigern takes firm control and runs the country like a quasi-dictator. Mind you, the Tūath kingdoms are very much unto themselves, and so it is not quite as what some historians make it out to be with Vortigern. When he screws up the agreement with the Saxons, he is quickly ousted from power—a trademark that is distinctly Celtic. By contrast, in the Saxons' hierarchy, when their leader Cerdic loses the battle of Badon, nothing happens to him. The Saxons were on a vicious gangster warlord system where the strongest called the shots. Anyone who did not like it was quickly beheaded.

At this time, a little geography of the country has to be described. The country has completely changed from what it looked like under Roman rule. Roman Britannia was nicely cut up into four main partitions, two in the north and two in the south. It was very easy to understand. Prior to this, Britannia it was the typical patchwork quilt of small, petty Celtic kingdoms. Each one had a very distinct identity to it from a political perspective, and of course it adds to the argument they were Iron Age people and not Celts. However, what has to be noted is the infrastructure was typically Celtic, but it was their mandate that made them unique.

To begin, you have to imagine for a moment a map of the United Kingdom in general and what it looked like prior to the Romans. I will try to point out some of the various Celtic tribes that stretched across the island. Starting down in the lower east side, in the region of Kent, you had the Cantii and Atrebates. These Briton Celts had a commercial relationship with the main continent of Europe. Trade was good, and they wanted to keep it that way. They were not particularly interested in getting into a losing fight with the Romans. If we move north-east into Essex, Suffolk and Norfolk, we come to the Trinovante and the Icenii Celts. The Romans recognized these two groups as commercially shrewd and private. They had no problems picking a fight with the Romans if they could profit from it. Moving west toward the Gloucestershire region, you have the Durotriges Celts. Almost nothing is written about this tribe, but based on the Corodicus rebellion, it is implied they were nationalists. Unfortunately, they did not seem to do well at any of the rebellions with which they got involved. Moving into Wales, we come across two groups, the Siluré and the Ordoviis. It is beyond certainty they were the most vicious with which the Romans had to contend. Going down to Cornwall were the Domnonii Celts. Like the Canttii, they had successful trade going on with the continent, operating out of Tintagel, and they were not about to jeopardize it fighting the Romans. Moving north into the central Yorkshire region, you have probably the largest and most politically influential tribal nation, the famed Briganté. Based on much of what the Roman Tacitus wrote about them, it would seem much of their time was spent in civil war. Going farther north into Northumbria, we have three groups left: the Novantae, the Selgorvae and the Votadinii. Sly and untrustworthy are the easiest ways to sum them up. As you can see, there is very little common ground with any of them to form a confederacy, as was the case in Gaul, Pictland and Scotti (Ireland).

The Picts, whom the Romans continuously underestimated, were divided into three main provincial nations: the Maeatae in the south by the Firth of Forth, the Calidonii in the centre and the Cornavii way off in the northern region, past the Ness. As mentioned before, the Ard-Ri sat in Inverness. The Picts were just as tough as the Silures but were a lot more organized.

Crossing the Irish Sea were the Scotti, or as the Romans called them, the Hybernians. They were explicitly Halstatt Celts who came up from Iberia (Spain). They did not border themselves according to tribal recognition, as was the case in the rest of the Celtic world, but on provincially named regions such as Leinster, Munster, Connaught and Ulster. It wasn't until about AD 100 that they established a central government system that operated out of the famed capital of Tara.

This is what the Celtic British and Irish islands looked like before the Romans arrived.

During Rome

Probably one of the most beautifully illustrated books on the Roman British period was done by Guy de la Bedoyère, *Roman Britain*. Guy went to great lengths to show what many of the homes and civitas looked like when the Romans occupied Britannia. Many of the houses had heated floors and washrooms, and the civitas had public baths. Living conditions in general were opulent compared to what they were before. Let's face it: it is a far cry from the Celtic small, round, thatched-roof huts. Hygiene was horrendous, to say the least.

Now, here comes the twist. If living conditions were so unbelievably improved, why did the Britons quickly return to their former society when the Romans left? The answer is for two reasons. First, those who were allowed this sumptuous lifestyle were a limited portion of the population. You may have succeeded, like the Cantii did, to be recognized as a Roman citizen, but you were not privileged to Roman culture. If you wanted the Roman lifestyle in the south-east portion of the country, then you had to move to Londinium. Obviously not too many Britons could afford to do that. The second reason, which was partly explained, is a substantial part of the country was what the Romans called "client states." This meant the original inhabitants were still running their own rural governments. The arrangement was that as long as the select indigenous population traded with the Romans, they could continue to run their own affairs. The Dumnonii, Silure, Ordovice, Brigante, Novantae, Selgorvae, Votadinii and Daminii were all client states of Rome. When you recall the areas they resided in, you will quickly see that almost half the country had been allowed to continue their old ways.

One of the best examples of what it looked like was in the south-east corner of Wales. Caerleon was in this region and proved to be an excellent example of how the Romans cohabited with their Briton neighbours, with an enormous garrison and civitas both together. Then just a few miles down the road, at Dinas Powy, the Silures Britons had their wooden fortress capital. This kind of setup was similar with the Dumonii and the Ordovices. Things were different when you got up by Hadrian's Wall. Here, the northern Britons were too close to the Picts, and so they were in a special arrangement with the Romans. Tribes like the Novantae and the Selgorvae were completely unto themselves and were being paid to help with security along Hadrian's Wall. If it was not understood before, client state tribes were not recognized as citizens of Rome but were more like political allies. Again, it made all the difference when the Romans finally left. The client state tribes had always been independent, and so there was no change with them either before, during or after the Roman occupation.

Now to see what kind of relationship existed between Roman Britannia and her client states.

Adrien Gilbert, who penned *The Holy Kingdom,* says Rome had been involved in one conflict after another in Briton right up to AD 112. When you consider their first permanent arrival was in AD 43, that works out to 69 years of continuous fighting with the locals. I am pretty sure the Romans were exhausted and were quite prepared to compromise to get just a little peace of mind. I know of two major events in this time that occurred. The first one was the Caratacus rebellion in Wales. This went on for seven years and forced the Romans to terms with the Silures. The next big one was in AD 61, with the fame Boudica rebellion. It only lasted for one year, but if the casualties reported are correct, the Romans had suffered over 90,000 dead when the rampage was over. Then in AD 71, the Romans were forced to send an army of two legions of regulars along with three auxiliaries to deal with those annoying Picts. This army was led by Roman General Agricola. He brought along with him his nephew Tacitus, who wrote a full account of the campaign. Agricola found himself in a four-year slugfest with the Picts, and in the end, he had to call it off. And to think this was only the open volley for the Romans! There were a lot more to come after this. When it came to the Britons and their unpredictable Celtic nature, the Romans were almost never at rest for the whole time they occupied the island.

The biggest Roman military mystery that still baffles historians today is the disappearance of the IX Legion. They know for a fact the legion was last stationed in northern Briton circa AD 120. Despite Agricola's exhausting campaign, the Romans were still suffering from continued attacks by the Picts. From the 2011 movie *The Eagle,* directed by Kevin MacDonald, the latest hypothesis is the legion was slaughtered by the Picts. It is not a bad argument considering that soon after the legion's disappearance, the Romans go through all the bother to build the infamous Hadrian's Wall. Hundreds of historians say that since the Romans could not defeat the Picts, the wall was the final solution. This tells us the conflict in Briton carried on still further in time.

To the Romans' disappointment, the wall did very little to stop the Picts. Frustrated even more, the Romans marched farther into

Pict territory, and in AD 142 they built the Antonine Wall at the Firth of Forth. It was made of wood and proved even more useless than Hadrian's Wall, and so in short order it was abandoned.

The most concerted effort to squash the Pictish problem once and for all came with Emperor Septimius Severus. In AD 208, he brought with him an overwhelming military army of four legions comprising of more than 40,000 soldiers. For the next three years, Severus personally directed the campaign against the Picts, and the results were even more staggering than before. Just like when Agricola was here, the Picts engaged in an extremely effect guerrilla warfare that claimed the lives of more than 50,000 Romans. Replacing the casualties was nothing short of a nightmare. Unfortunately for the soldiers, the causalities only made Severus's resolve stronger. The war against the Picts was an ancient version of the American Vietnam War. Lucky for the Romans, in AD 211 the emperor fell ill and soon died. His son Caracalla, who endured the military fiasco with his father, was quick to pack up the camp and race home.

I suppose that because the next big campaign doesn't happen till AD 365, it would appear at long last there was a degree of overdue tranquillity on the island. This is when the Roman Britons finally started to build those magnificent homes that are described in Guy de la Bedoyère's book. However, just when things are beginning to get back to normal, all hell lets loose yet again.

Historians call it the Great Conspiracy. The reason for the title is because various Roman units helped participate in the largest Irish/Pict attack in the history of Briton. Roman historians claim that the combined forces of the two barbarian armies added up to more than 100,000. They swept over the wall and penetrated as far south as Londinium itself. For the Irish, I know from the *Chronicles of the Four Masters* that they were led by a man name Crymthann, a Fianna warrior from Connaught. What is known of the man is that he was an exceptionally skilled warrior, and so him leading the Irish to the wall of Londinium is not surprising. The Picts were led by a brilliant tactician, King Gartnait II, who managed to persuade the Saxons to come along in the venture. The unfortunate aspect of the massive assault was that it turned into one big orgy of looting. There was no effort to conquer or re-establish the Celtic kingdoms or to remove the Romans, which they could have done had they decided to re-establish ties with the Briton Celts. Three years later, Roman

General Theodosius arrives with two crack Roman legions, and in less than a year, he pushes the invaders back over the wall. As for the Roman traitors, it goes without saying they were severely dealt with. The standard punishment for mutiny in the Roman army was decimation: every 10th man in the legion was executed.

By AD 410, the Irish and the Picts, like the rest of the known world, were well aware that the Roman Empire was falling apart. For the Irish in particular, a brilliant young warrior comes to the Tara throne. His name is Niall MacEochaid (son of King Eochaid, married to the Saxon princess Caren), but he was commonly known as the great Niall of the Nine Hostages. There is a wealth of information on this extraordinary young leader in the *Annals of Ulster* and the *Chronicles of the Four Masters.* Yet outside of Ireland, almost nothing is known about him. The archaeological evidence of his success is indirectly credited by numerous British and Welsh sources. Niall's father had provided him an impressive navy of more than 400 small war ships with an average crew of about 40 sailors. With this armada, as St. Patrick testified, he could sweep down on large Roman civitas and capture 2,000 Roman slaves. It turns out Niall was not interested in just getting slaves for Ireland. His big ambition was empire building—a subject the Irish would never have imagined was possible. Oddly enough, it is British academic authorities and writers, like Mike Ash in *King Arthur,* who verified the Irish conquest of western Briton. According to Adrian Gilbert, the Ogham stones found in Scotland, Wales, Cornwall and Brittany verified that the Irish campaign was in fact true.

Niall started his campaign in Scotland, and when he came to Wales, he ran into Roman General Magnus Maximus circa AD 385. Niall didn't do so well fighting him in Wales, but he was a little more successful when he retreated to Northumbria. Magnus apparently had bigger political plans than trying to contain the Irish renegade, and so he soon took off with a sizable portion of the Roman forces to Gaul, where he usurped Western Roman Emperor Gratian. With Magnus gone, Niall returned to the task at hand of devouring the Britons. He took firm control of Ordovices and then moved onto Demetae. Circa AD 395, Niall comes face-to-face with Flavius Stilicho. From what the Roman writers tell us, Stilicho found fighting Niall an unusual challenge. Normally the Romans could steamroll the Celts like they did to Boudica, but not with Niall. Stilicho had to bring all the remaining Roman forces into a central location near the Deva (Chester) garrison to keep the Irish at bay. Again, like Magnus, Stilicho had ambitions and wanted to pursue elsewhere; like his predecessor, he pulled another sizable force to Gaul and was gone.

Niall was basically all alone now, and so he opened up his Dumnonia (Cornwall) front. According to *The Annals of the Four Masters,* Niall took all of Dumnonia by the end of AD 405. Now, something has to be mentioned here because I am sure many will be confused that such an enormous conquest had occurred, and yet there is no record of it. The reason for this is the Celts did not conquer in the typical Roman fashion; this will come up again when we start to get into Arthur's reign. There is a poem about Niall taking Scotland in one day and without killing so much as a single person. If you are familiar with the poem, then you are aware of how he did it. The way it happened was like this.

When a king lost a battle to his enemy, that did not necessarily mean he lost his kingdom. The common practice was that the losing king would submit by way of tribute and royal hostages to the winning king. This would demonstrate his new allegiance to the victor. Thus, the kingdom borders would not change but were now added to the winning kingdom. Under this typical practice, Dumnonia is now a subject kingdom to Ireland. By understanding this, you will now realise the significance to Niall's nickname, Niall of the Nine Hostages. Niall had taken over nine kingdoms in his lifetime. Ireland as we know it has only three kingdoms,[1] and so we know he had to have taken over other kingdoms outside Ireland to have been given the title of "Nine Hostages." From the *Annals of Ulster,* I figure that in order to have accumulated nine countries, Niall was in possession of Northumbria, Gwynedd, Dyfed, Brittany, Pictland, Dalriada and the three Irish kingdoms.

As we know, Roman Britannia was partly made up with a series of small client kingdoms, and despite what people like Tacitus wrote, on many occasions there was still strong local resistance, particularly from the Silures. The Silures, like the Picts, were a tough people. Niall had a difficult time fighting them. His little trick he used on the Picts wasn't working with the southern kingdoms. A Roman Britain

---

[1]   There are actually only four kingdoms in Ireland. Meath does not count as a kingdom due to where the Ard-Ri resides.

named Constantine II (c. AD 403) is said to have operated out of the Roman garrison of Isca (Caerleon). He had at his disposal one of the last remaining professional Roman legions. An incident occurred in the Silures region against the Irish, of which the historical details are very light. It had to have been a sizable problem because Constantine ended up needing a full legion to address it. There is no doubt the Silures themselves were involved. Assuming they could at least put into the field 5,000 men, we have a combined force of more than 10,000 men. It was a major event at the time. Anyway, whatever became of the armed engagement, Constantine was triumphant. He became a hero overnight and was hailed by his men as the new emperor of Britannia. Word of his success quickly reached Gaul, and the Romans down there called for his help in dealing with the Franks and Visigoths, who had recently invaded Roman Spain. He took the remaining legion and marched into Spain. From here, it is recorded he was ambushed—by whom, we don't know—and was killed in the disaster.

A King Arthur note has to be made at this point on Constantine II. This is the Constantine whom Geoffrey of Monmouth is talking about as Uther's father. In his fabricated pedigree, he draws a family tree with Constantine at the top, then Uther and finally Arthur. He creates the impression that Arthur is related to Constantine II, which is completely false. Also, this Constantine gets confused with the second Constantine, who is mentioned by Gildas, who became the ruler of Dumnonia after King Geraint (c. AD 517), so there are two of them. The first one is Roman, and the second on is Dumnonian Celt. I talk more about the second Constantine later, in chapter 8.

Circa AD 410, the famous letter to Emperor Honorius was sent by the civilian civitas authorities for military help. As everyone in Britain is well aware, the answer came back as no. Britannia was now completely on its own. Shortly after this, a major revolt broke out, and all the Roman officials caught the first boat off the island and formally ended Roman control of the country. The garrisons were empty, Hadrian's Wall was abandoned, and the administrators were sailing for the continent. For about the next 10 years, there is silence across the land. However, *The Annals of the Four Masters* is spilling over with all the activities of Niall of the Nine Hostages.

After Rome will be addressed fully in the next chapter.

4

Briton Returns

> Woe unto the Red Dragon, for his extermination
> draweth nigh; and his caverns shall be occupied of
> the White Dragon that betokeneth the Saxons whom
> thou hast invited hither. But the Red signifieth the
> race of Britain that shall be oppressed of the White.
> Therefore shall the mountains and the valleys
> thereof be made level plain and the streams of the
> valleys shall flow with blood
>
> —a Merlin quote from Geoffrey of Monmouth's works

Technically, the Dark Ages begin with the crossing of the Rhine in AD 405 of five Germanic nations (Franks, Alans, Burgundians, Saxons and Vandals) into Roman Gaul. From the south via Greece were the Visigoth under Alaric, who were on the move to sack Rome itself. At this point, the Western Empire rapidly disintegrates. It is at this time that Celtic Briton re-emerges.

Somewhere between AD 410 and AD 415, Niall of the Nine Hostages was assassinated near the River Loire in Gaul by one of his own men. With him died a legend that could very well have been bigger than any story of King Arthur. The *Four Masters* fully indicates that no sooner did the assassination occur than there was a mad scramble to get Niall's body back to Ireland. It's not known whom the Irish (Confederacy) were fighting, but likely it was the Franks or the Visigoths. Whoever it was, they knew the Irish king was dead, and they were onto them. Niall was successfully returned to Ireland

and was buried about 20 kilometres north-west of Armagh. He was quickly replaced by his brother Nath I mac Fiachrach. It would appear the Druids of Tara were aware of Niall's accomplishments, and so the traditional elections of a new king were temporarily suspended, as far as we know.

According to Tim Clarkson in *The Makers of Scotland,* the events that transpired in Pictland (Scotland) after the death of Niall were also immediate. It would appear in those days bad news travelled very fast. The *Four Masters* tells us no sooner did Nath come to the throne than the Picts declared their independence. Nath wasted no time and sailed an army to Caledonia. For the next 10 years or so, the Scotti (Irish) were embroiled in a vicious war with the Picts. Some say the reason Nath pursued this relentless, bloody bath was inherited from his mother, Mongfind, from Eochaid's first marriage. She was said to be the scariest woman to ever walk the streets of Tara. Even so, the Picts had elected themselves a very capable leader as well. His name was Drest of a Hundred Battles. Remarkably, according to the *Pictish Chronicles,* Drest is alleged to have never lost a battle. This will be seen as puzzling when in real time there are a limited amount of sources to validate it.

The person who gives us probably the best clue of what was really going on in northern Briton is none other than King Coel Hen (Old King Coel). (Yes, this is the man the famous nursery rhyme comes from.) King Coel was the first ruler of the newly-formed kingdom of Rheged. It used to be Brigante up until the Romans left. It is actually from the *Welsh Triads* that we learn of the events that transpired in Rheged at this time. Like the Picts, once King Coel heard of Niall's death, he too withdrew his loyalty to the Scotti. The Scotti Empire was dwindling in size as fast as it was created. Reminds you of Germany in the World Wars, doesn't it?

The fighting between the Picts and the Scotti spilled over into Gododdin in approximately AD 420. Gododdin, like many of new Dark Ages kingdoms, came into existence from another alliance from three former Celtic nations: the Votadinii, the Novantii and the Selgorvaes. Their capital became Dun Eideann (Edinburgh). Nath I mac Fiachrach appears to have been making gains even though the Picts say he lost every battle. The Scotti territory by AD 425 stretched up the western coast of Pictland and now moved south into Rheged itself. It is at this time King Coel, who really is no longer capable of leading an army into battle, takes a disastrous risk. He decides to attack the Scotti. The results were that both the Picts and the Scotti pounced on him. Overnight the short-lived Rheged Kingdom disappears from existence. However, events are so fluid in the Dark Ages that we find King Coel is allowed to return to power circa AD 435.

Chris Barber, *in King Arthur: The Mystery Unraveled,* tells us that Coel's restoration was not a coincidence. The Ard-Ri Nath dies in AD 435, and an Ard-Ri Loegaire (pronounced *Leary*) replaces him. We now have to go to the *Annals of Ulster* to continue the story. Loegaire is the son of Niall, but he is unfortunately sidetracked from pursuing the ambitions of his father on account of the arrival of Saint Patrick. As I am sure the whole world knows, when Saint Patrick arrived in Ireland circa AD 436 as a bishop, he had a powerful impact on the country. Christianity swept across the land at an incredible pace. Loegaire, who should have been paying attention to what was happening in Rheged, was for the most part consumed with internal affairs. He was furious when he discovered that even his own two daughters, Eithne the fair and Fedelelm the red, had become Christians.

If Saint Patrick wasn't enough to keep Loegaire busy, he added in a personal grudge he had with the provincial kingdom of Leinster. Leinster is from where the assassin of Niall came because it was Loegaire out for revenge. He launched an ill-planned attack on the province and stumbled into an ambush. His army was badly defeated, and he was taken prisoner. Lucky for Loegaire, the king of Leinster was not too happy with the country converting to Christianity. As it was, Loegaire was quickly returned to Tara on a geis[2] he would never take up arms against Leinster again.

From Welsh sources like the *Welsh Triads,* we find out how fast Niall's empire collapses. Pictland was the first to withdraw from its oath to Niall, then Rheged (Brigante) and finally Dumnonii. There is no mention of Brittany, but it can be assumed the country returned to its own the moment the Scotti army withdrew with Niall's body. Another technical point must be mentioned, and that is on all the hostages who were captured by Niall. Whatever happen to them? In reality, they were probably let go. There is also the issue when a

---

[2] A "geis" is a Celtic pagan curse to guarantee a person will not violate a promise.

new king comes to power from one of the hostage countries, such as Dumnonii. If the king is elected and is not related to the former king, then the hostages are of no value anymore. The allegiance naturally falls apart, and this happened a lot not only in Briton but throughout the whole of Europe.

Speaking of Scotti, a name change was starting to take place at about this time in Ireland. The Scottis no longer referred to themselves as Scotti but were now using the identity of Irish. However, this was a very slow process. In Ulster, it did not go over well at all. They kept to their Scotti heritage right up to AD 700, when it became an entity onto itself as Scotland. Knowing this, the reader must be conscious of it, for from here on in, there will be a fair bit of bouncing around with the names. What may help is in Pictland, the term *Scot* replaces the former *Scotii*. Thus by the 8th century, we have what we recognize today as the Scots and Irish representing Scotland and Ireland, respectively.

In AD 426, there is another political lull from all the headaches by the Scotti; mind you, the raids for slaves weren't affected. However, the major invasion aspects had dramatically subsided. It is at this time in Powy that a man by the infamous name Vortigern comes to power. Powy is another newly developed nation that was created from the Celtic state of Ordovices. There is no explanation I have come across on how this happens; not even Timothy Venning, who wrote *Kings and Queens of Wales,* can provide a suitable answer. Whatever the events were, the result is a new kingdom was formed, and at its head was Vortigern.

Right from the get-go, Vortigern is handicapped by the facts that he can only speak Goidelic Gaelic and that his background is Ordovices Scotti. Everybody in Powy is Brethonic Briton, and so this has a natural problem at its base. Yet despite his limitations, he proves to be a skilful tactician and a ferocious Celtic warrior by nature. British historians paint him as not only aggressive but also ruthless. Within a year of him coming to power, he expands the borders of Powy to stretch across the centre of Wales, reaching the Roman civita of Viroconium (Wroxeter). This beautiful Roman centre inspires him to move his capital from Unys Emery, near Anglesey, to Viroconium. It is here that he runs into the Roman Briton Ambrosius Aurelianus, who like himself is ambitious to redefine Briton as a new, unified nation but with a Roman twist to it. Vortigern is not impressed, and soon the two are at each other's throats. It's implied but not confirmed that the two engage in an armed conflict. Unfortunately, Ambrosius does not fare well in the outcome and is forced to flee into exile to Brittany.

Chasing Ambrosius out of the country must have been one of the most amazing accomplishments for Vortigern, on top of the fact that he made Powy once of the largest new countries in Briton. He was probably in an extreme sense of euphoria, which prompted him to take the next big challenge: unifying the country.

With the fall of Rheged to the Irish and the Picts, Vortigern got his first reality check that these countries were still very powerful. It was clear if there was any hope for establishing himself as a central figure to the unification of the Britons, it would have to be through the Celtic system of an elected Ard-Ri. Timothy Venning uses the term *Ynys Prieden* as the name of the new Briton confederacy union. I assume he got the name from the *Welsh Annals*.

In order to entertain the subject of Ard-Ri, we have to review what Britannia now looks like after Roman withdrawal. The island has, for the most part, been under the empire for more than 300 years. Many people were now what would be recognized as Romans, yet as we know, the client states were still very much Celtic. The reason for looking at this is because the Roman Britons had long since lost their ability to fight. It was the Celtic Britons who were still warrior in nature and capable of defending the country from invaders. This becomes a crucial point to the survival of the island.

It was recorded in the *Welsh Annals* that the Cantii were violently upset that Vortigern gave away their nation to the Anglo-Saxons in AD 449, and so it would appear the Romans had allowed them to be a client state. However, the Incenii and the Trinovantes had been fully submerged into the Roman culture, and so they no longer understood the Ard-Ri system. The Durotriges at the mouth of the Severn had also been lost to the Romans, and so they are out of the equation as well. After this, though, it is completely different. The Brigantes (Rheged) is Celtic, and all the tribes of Wales—the Silures, the (Irish) Ordovices, the Irish Demetae and Glywysyng (Glamorgan and Gwent)—are Celtic. Dumnonia is not only Celtic but is still politically fully intact from its pre-Roman days. Way up north, under Irish control, was Gododdin, and it too was completely Celtic. Thus, when it was said and done, Briton was still about two-thirds

Celtic. Therefore, introducing the Ard-Ri kind of government is not a farfetched idea. The theory is proven because Vortigern doesn't have any difficulty quickly assembling the Briton confederacy of Ynys Prydein.

It is at this moment you have people like Chris Barber and Rodney Castleden arguing that the name Vortigern means leader, and that it isn't his real name. I looked into this and found there were about a half dozen different names people have claimed were his real name. There was so many of them that it was not hard for me to dismiss the whole subject. Then to make sure what I was doing was correct, I reviewed the *Annals of Ulster* of the Irish system to compare. The appointment of Ard-Ri is like saying someone is king; the title never changes. For example, Eochaid was an Ard Ri, Niall MacEochaid was an Ard-Ri, Crymthann was an Ard-Ri and finally Nath I mac Fiachrach was an Ard-Ri. As you can see, the title Ard-Ri is consistent. This does not hold true for Briton. After Vortigern comes Vortimor, then Ambrosius, then Geraint and finally Arthur. If the name was a title, it would be consistent, but it is not. Some play with the title of Pendragon as being the word for king. However, when you research this, you find the factious character Uther is the only one with this illustrious title. Arthur in his legend is given the Pendragon title, but not in his real life. Therefore, it seemed to me, based on the way the Britons behaved previous to the coming of the Romans, that they had come up with an Ard-Ri office, but they did not want to call him an Ard-Ri. What the Britons wanted was that once there was no need for a supreme leader, they wanted to be able to quickly get rid of him. From what Bede and Nennius tell us, this certainly was the case after the Battle of Badon. From the historical records, Arthur quickly disappears. It is only through the legendary tales that Arthur continues to be the Ard-Ri of Ynys Prydein. This kind of methodology was not all that unusual if you take a fast look at Germania in the first century. When Arminius defeated the Romans in AD 7, the Germans celebrated the victory, but the next day the confederacy was terminated, and Arminius returned to being a farmer.

The historians Jack Whyte and Francis Pryor allude to the idea that once Vortigern was appointed to the head of the Ynys Pryden, he had several centres of operations. The first one was Vecuronium (Wroxeter), and the second one was Camolud (Colchester). The point is there was no specific capital of the new Briton nation. In other

words, all the excitement about there being a Camelot somewhere in Briton was pure fiction. Once more the subject was yet another fabrication by Geoffrey of Monmouth. When Arthur at last comes along, an assembly area does appear to have existed, but it was of a non-permanent nature, as the confederacy itself was.

Vortigern's Irish heritage proved to be useful when it came to at least partly solving the Irish-Pict dilemma. The Britons had lost almost half of their land to the Halstatt invaders. Further, the Britons were not capable of fighting both at the same time. Though Nath and Drest were at each other's throats for most of the time, Rheged proved they would, on a moment's notice, quickly collaborate against the Britons. Therefore, Vortigern had to come up with a scheme that would isolate at least one of them. It turned out he came up with a brilliant plan. Because he was fluent in Goedelic Gaelic, it was easy for him to have his daughter Scthmore marry Loegaire's son Fedelmid in AD 429. Apparently, the scheme worked. The Scotti were immediately taken out of the equation, and the Picts were left to fend for themselves. For the time being, Vortigern's tenuous confederacy remained intact. However, as numerous chronicles of the time showed, the Irish alliance was shaky at best, and the Picts under Drest were still far too powerful on their own. Vortigern still needed a plan B.

The peace lasted until about AD 446, when Loegaire once again started allowing Scotti pirates to raid Briton's west coast. The way Loegaire looked at it was much the same way as Queen Elizabeth I (from the 16th century) viewed Sir Francis Drake. The pirate raids were independent actions of their own; they were not actions of the nation even though everyone knew whom the pirates represented. Vortigern was put under enormous pressure to deal with this if he had any hope of staying in power. From what is surmised, Vortigern knew instinctively that if he took any action against the Scotti, they would quickly join with the Picts again, and he would be right back where he started. As everyone in the British Isles, and quite possibly the whole world, knows, his plan B turned out to be to ask the Anglos, Jutes, and Saxons for help. In AD 449, Hengist and Horsa, leading the tri-Germanic entourage, arrive in Briton in three ships, responding to the plea. Unfortunately for Vortigern, this plan badly backfires.

When Loegaire gets news of the Saxon and Briton collusion, he is outraged and immediately declares war. However, we find from his

internal problems that he hasn't got much to work with anymore. For one, Leinster is not interested in going to war with the Britons again; they had their fill with Niall and want nothing to do with it. Second, circa AD 439, a man by the name of Cunedda from Gododdin came into Scotti-Irish Ordovices territory and kicked them out. Finally, the ongoing conflict with the Picts had drained the country's resources as a whole, and Ireland simply didn't have the fighting power anymore. It took Loegaire a good 10 years to muster a sizable force to match the combined forces of the Britons and Saxons. Numerous sources say in AD 460, the Scotti manage to put a force together that caused some real concerns for the Britons.

However, at this same point in time, the Britons were hardly concerned with the Scotti and Picts. The Anglo, Jute, and Saxon alliance had dissolved. According to Constantius, Bishop Germanus's historian, Hengist and Drest met in two distinct battles that ended in stalemates. As it was, Hengist was impressed with the Pictish fighting capability and decided to have a truce with them. This truce was kept from Vortigern's knowledge. Vortigern was fooled into believing the engagements were both Saxon victories, and so he was quite prepared to reward them for their successes. Hengist took full advantage of the situation, and his demands were nothing short of extravagant. He demanded land and gold as payment for his efforts, and he got both. The entire nation of Cantii was turned over to the Saxons.

The *Anglo-Saxon Chronicles* gives us a wealth of detail on the debacle of Vortigern's relationship with the Saxons. Circa AD 462 is when it all comes to a boil. The Saxons invite the kings and princes of Briton nations to a special feast on Salisbury Plains. Nobody is to be armed. However, the Saxons were armed, and on command they came out and killed all the Britons except Vortigern. He was spared because he had married Hengist's beautiful daughter, Rowena. When Vortigern returned to the shambled alliance of Briton in Viruconium, he was immediately ousted from office. His son Vortimor took over and was quick to go after the Saxons. We have to rely on Nennius and Bede to tell us what happened next. Vortimor was exceptional and drove the Saxons out of Lyncoln. In four major battles, he forced the Saxons back to the island of Thanet, just off the east coast of Cantii (Kent). Unfortunately, the fourth battle proved to be fatal, and Vortimor was killed.

When all this is going on, Vortigern makes for the hills. He heads to the former Ordovice's capital of Dnys Emrys in the Snowdonia Mountains. Circa 465, Ambrosius Aurelianus returns from exile in Brittany and goes straight for Dnys Emrys. He lays siege to the Celtic fortress and burns it to the ground with Vortigern in it. Thus ends the legacy of Vortigern. For the next 10 years, Ambrosius is locked in a vicious conflict with the Saxons. They had called for help back in Denmark, and a sizable force came to their aid. Bede, who is particularly generous in heaping accolades on Ambrosius, claims the Roman Britain won all his battles and restored Briton to much of her former days. Then Anglo-Saxon treachery strikes again. An assassin is sent to his army camp, and Ambrosius is killed by poisoning.

A King Geraint of Dumonia is elected as the next Ard-Ri to Unys Pridein.

5

Chronicles, Annals, Pedigrees and Bardic Poems

Everyone is a moon, and has a dark side which he never shows to anybody.

—Mark Twain

The background setting for King Arthur is mostly in place. Only one more point has to be covered before we at last delve into the man himself, and that is the literature.

One of the things I discovered about King Arthur was the enormous amount of documents that exist on the man—and I am not talking about the legendary material. This subject is nothing short of staggering. Apparently from legitimate sources of Dark Ages Briton, King Arthur is mentioned a lot. In chapter 1, I last left with the names of three historians who were the foundations to the writers of the 12th century: Gildas (early 6th century), Bede the Venerable (late 8th century) and Nennius (early 9th century). These men were monks from the Celtic Christian movement that swept most of the British Isles at the time. Modern British historians give you the impression, through their interpretation, that these three men were basically all the same when referencing the historical Arthur. Further, they would have you believe that because of the Dark Ages, writing and literature in general had all but disappeared. On these two points, if I can quote one of Britain's leading experts in archaeology and history, Francis Pryor, "It's all complete rubbish!"

Francis Pryor did a rather lengthy BBC documentary on the age of King Arthur from an archaeological perspective. One of the most interesting aspects of the TV special was his research into the Celtic Christian Ogham Stones. These stones dominated much of the western coast of Britain, starting in Wales and going down to the very tip of Cornwall. The stones were introduced to the Britons by the Irish in the late 4th century strictly as pagan landmarks. They average about 2.0 metres high, with a 0.3-metre-wide face and 0.15-metres in thickness. I uncovered there are about 300 or so of these pagan-era stones still in existence. All along the edges of the stones are found small notches or markings that make up the Celtic lettering known as Ogham. In the middle of the 5th century, more of the same kinds of stones appeared, but with a very Christian addition to them. The Defynnog Stone in Defynnog, Maescar, Powys, is an example of Christian inclusion on the Celtic stone. On the top is found the Ogham lettering, and on the bottom is the Christian cross. In the centre is Latin lettering. The lettering spells out the name of a person, and that same name is reflected in the Ogham lettering, so it's strictly a translation. The Ogham is found on just about every stone in the Christian age, which tells you that Gaelic was still the dominant language of the country. Latin is just starting to make its breakthrough. What Francis Pryor thought particularly fascinating about these stones in a number of cases was when there was any descriptions or message written, it was done in verse, not prose.[3] That style of writing indicates a very sophisticated society. Francis is pointing that when the Romans left, the Britons' light of literature did not go out with them. Briton was still an academically advanced society. It will be later discussed just how advanced they were once the monastic movement gets going.

---

[3] Prose is the normal way of writing; verse is poetic, stylized writing. For example, Shakespeare wrote in verse. Newspapers write in prose.

C. Donoghue

"Ogham Stone Column"

The Christian movement in the British Isles is a remarkable subject unto itself. According to Adrian Gilbert in *The Holy Kingdom*, Christianity had a much earlier ecclesiastical establishment in this country than anywhere else in Europe. As a result, a foundation for an advanced education to a commoner was founded here first. Again, this phenomenon will be explained later. Adrian claims the Christian movement was well under way in the 1st century of Roman Britannia. He implies that Saint Patrick was not the original revolutionary of the Christian movement as he is credited. There is some merit to what he says is true. Patrick came to Ireland as a bishop, not a priest, which is a clue onto itself. The Church would not have sent a bishop if there were no churches already present. Adrian strongly feels the spread of Christianity in the British Islands was instigated by Joseph of Arimathea. In Wales he is called Saint Ilid. Justin E. Griffin, in his *Glastonbury and the Grail*, supports this observation as well (with reservations).

Other than in the Llandaff Charter, there is no evidence Joseph of Arimathea was ever in Briton.

The spread of Christianity really took off in the late 5th century, but not in the conventional sense with churches and cathedrals. It was the monastic movement that really promoted the Christian religion in the British Islands. The centre of monasticism was found in Ireland

and not in Briton. It flourished at an astonishing rate, such that the Irish were exporting monks at the beginning of the 5th century to Briton. Monasticism was briefly a type of humble, communal, solitary lifestyle totally devoted to the worship of the Christian god. The participants were of course called monks. It was a hard life to live, but there was some major benefits to it, namely education. Learning was probably one of the biggest drawbacks to the Celtic world. It was solely controlled by the Druids, and only a select few were privileged to it. Irish scholars claim Druidism survived best in Ireland, right up to the end of the 6th century. The average Irish monk could speak three languages (Gaelic, Latin and Greek), which demonstrated the thirst for knowledge was extreme. The denial of knowledge by the Druids was a critical element to the massive success of the monastic identity. People flocked to the movement to learn things they never knew possible before. In Briton, the average monk could only speak two languages, Gaelic and Latin.

It was the Irish who were the centre of the educational aspect of the monastic movement. All of the largest educational institutions were of Irish origins; Clonmacnoise, Bangor, Kells and Iona were examples of their system. Here, thousands of students came in from all over Europe. Each of these centres had great scriptorium centres producing hundreds of books. From the Viking Age in the 10th century, the average count was in excess of 800 books per monastery. Currently at Trinity College in Dublin, there are approximately a dozen books that have survived from this period, and you can see the work involved was nothing short of incredible. The pages in the books were more works of art then just writing. One of the finest examples of this was the famous Book of Kells. Writing exploded all over the British and Irish Isles on a variety of topics, not just religion.

Francis Pryor's observation of the high academic standard that was now in both islands is supported by numerous other historians like Mike Ash, Christopher Gidlow, Rodney Castleden, Jean Markale and Norma Goodwich. Goodwich has an added interesting twist on the academic profile, in that the sheer volume of the fictional writing alone supports the premise that King Arthur was real. The actual writings on King Arthur didn't take form until the 7th century; up until then, it was all in Bardic oral tradition. However, once finally put to paper, it was an exceptional level of quality—a point even Lady Charlotte Guest addresses when she put together a collection of

Welsh folklore stories in 1839. The stories have a verse infrastructure to them, meaning the sophistication was quite high.

Another interesting aspect that comes from the high sophistication is no longer relying wholly on Gildas, Bede and Nennius for the proof of King Arthur. With other sources now being of equal value, this makes the three principle monks insufficient references. This is a particularly important point to note if you are going to show any respect to Francis Pryor and Norma Goodwich's research. Further, those who restrict themselves to these three men will find only Nennius says Arthur fought at the Battle of Badon. With only one person being recognized as the sole authority to Arthur's existence, the case is extremely weak. Those who stand on this alone are blatantly ignorant of the latest research revelations by British archaeologists such as Francis Pryor. He alone has uncovered a wealth of new evidence that can substantiate much further than Nennius the existence of the Camelot Arthur. Such evidence cannot be ignored.

Further, when you take a moment and examine what scholars have clung to with these three monks, it turns out they are not qualitative historical sources to begin with. The books they compiled were more designed to promote the Christian religion than writing historical facts. They are absorbed in the damnation of royal tyrants rather than simply reflecting historical events. As it is, the text is very hard to read. I personally attempted to read Bede's *Historia Ecclesiastica Gentis Anglorum* (*Ecclesiastical History of the English People*). Once I arrived at the 40th page, I had to put it down. The diatribe was simply too much to handle. The name of the book does not reflect the majority of the content. Gildas, who was the first, wrote *De Excidio et Conquestu Britanniae* (*On the Ruin and Conquest of Britain*). This book is not as bad as Bede's, but its sermon-like writing style does try one's patience after a while. Lastly, there is Nennius. He wrote *Historia Brittonium* (*The History of the Britons*). Again, I admittedly didn't get very far into this book because his over-the-top, pious approach is irritating as well. Why modern historians stay with these three men as a primary source to the authentication of King Arthur is difficult to understand.

Norma Goodwich's line of thinking is where this part of the story is going to continue. She takes the position—and I completely agree with it—that there are other sources to consider besides the conventional ones when it comes to King Arthur. She feels the fictional stories on Arthur have merit in themselves to reveal there was an authentic Camelot king. In the same spirit, I feel the material that was either oral tradition told or written in the provincial Tuath kingdoms have merit. All across Briton, Wales and Cornwall, each of the kingdoms had their own scribes and bards that recorded the local events. For the most part, they followed the Celtic bard format of exaggeration when it came to recording events. The *Y-Gododdin* is a good example of this. Of course, it is recognized that the exaggerated nature of the bardic format makes it difficult to accept them as fact. However, I don't find it any more unacceptable than the religious diatribe that comes from the three monks. If their material should be considered, than so too should everybody else. Again, what we are looking for is the timeline, the places and the names. The story does matter because we know the embellishment was created so that the person would be remembered.

Now, let's examine some of the examples.

As mentioned, outside the ecclesiastical centres were the different small kingdoms that peppered the countryside. As we have learned, they were all Celtic in nature, and so their operations followed a Celtic infrastructure. The Celtic kings were no different in their vanity than any Norman or Saxon king who came after them. They typically wanted attention in areas of heritage and praise. Writing was not fully adopted until the 7th century, and so the king's glories were preserved through the bards and the Druids by means of oral tradition. The way it was done was creating poems or rhymes on everything. To verify whether these poems actually worked, one of the best examples to the claim is the famous nursery rhyme "London Bridge Is Falling Down." This little nursery rhyme was created in the 11th century when the Vikings came to London and tore down the bridges to make way for their longships. Think about it. It has remained perfectly intact for more than a thousand years. It shows that when the monks at last started writing down the various poems in the 7th century from oral tradition, nothing had changed. Many of the monks like Gildas, who were of Celtic Briton origins, would instantly know to record the bard poems precisely as they heard them. If he made any changes, the common person would know immediately it was not the same. It is from this that the monks were forced into writing it exactly the way people were saying it.

London Bridge is falling down,
Falling down, falling down.
London Bridge is falling down,
My fair lady.
London Bridge is broken down,
Broken down, broken down.
London Bridge is broken down,
My fair lady.

Build it up with wood and clay,
Wood and clay, wood and clay,
Build it up with wood and clay,
My fair lady.

The person who was adamant on this issue was Lady Guest. She had studied Welsh Celtic bards for a very long time and was able to determine whether a bard was genuine. Jean Markale, in *King of the Celts,* also emphasizes this point as well. For an expert, distinguishing a Celtic bard was as easy as being able to recognize a Shakespearian play. As we can see, there is merit to oral tradition because it can't be changed without someone knowing it, both when it was first recorded in writing and even today. Like music, we know instinctively how the lyrics go, and even the best experts are not going to fool anyone in changing them.

When I get older losing my hair
Many years from now
Will you still be sending me a valentine …

—Beatles, "When I'm Sixty-four"

Now that we have a grasp on the method of early recording, the next stage is what was recorded. It turns out this part is not difficult at all. First all, the kings wanted authentication as legitimate rulers. This was done by means of a royal genealogy, commonly known as a pedigree. It was very important to them that their places in history were perfectly recorded. Often it was dangerous to mess with this subject. An illegitimate king or queen would normally lead to a civil war. The best example to this is Empress Matilda of England in 1135, who had been usurped by her cousin Stephen of Blois. She couldn't do anything about it because it was on record that he was the king. She did try to press her claim, but it plunged the country into civil war for the next 10 years.

The second piece of record that kings insisted on was keeping track of their daily activities. This subject is referred to as the daily annals. Land grants were probably one of their most important daily functions, next to ceremonies. Kings wanted this to be completely accurate in the event of fraud. The Llandaff Charter shows how the Church made extra sure that when they got a land grant, they recorded it carefully. Thus it was doubly certain the king did as well. What's the point to all this? The answer comes with whose name is recorded and when. The Llandaff Charter has a King Arthur registered in several of the entries, and all are dated to the end of the 5th century. It naturally begs the curiosity: Is this the same Arthur of Badon? The timeline certainly fits. And if it is, then how did Gildas miss him? Not once does he mention the name of the king of his kingdom of Glywysing.

The *Tigernach Annals* in Ireland are said to be the most tedious of them all when it came to daily recording. It is because this chronology came into existence as a sort of a summary of events. Chronologies were often the text used at special ceremonies, like the appointing of a new king, to give a brief outline on the past glory of the kingdom. It was so much easier than going through the lengthy details of the annals.

These three institutional records systems were the mainstay of the Briton kingdom. When the bards were replaced by scribes, the oral tradition was now written down. What is certain is that the transfer of the material was precise. As stated, any misrepresentation in the transferring medium was likely a dangerous situation. If the oral tradition claimed there was a King Smith in 200 BC, then the scribe knew he had better write it down exactly that way. As mentioned, the written records did not get into full swing till the end of the 7th century. Up until then, only a select number of Kingdoms like eastern Powy, which had a Roman literary past, was fortunate to have one of the oldest records in the land. Remember, though it may have been written down in the 7th century, it was dangerous to try to alter the original records from the historical oral tradition kept by the Druids. A small example on this point is the Ard-Ri Cormac Mc Airt, of Ireland. He is precisely dated as being the High King of Ireland from AD 226 to 262. It was not until the 9th century that this was formally written down on parchment. Up until then, the records were kept by the Druids through oral tradition. Today, no one questions the legitimacy of these dates. It thus proves the methodology of oral tradition is well-founded.

There were some natural mistakes with the various entries on some kingdoms and religious centres, particularly when it came to recording the events of the neighbouring kingdom's activities. The reason for this is because events outside the main kingdom were unimportant. The activities of outside kingdoms were used more as a point of reference rather than a real source of specifics. I found this to be a particularly interesting point when outside kingdoms tried to record the pedigrees of the neighbouring kingdom. More often than not, they were wrong. Then there were people like Geoffrey of Monmouth, who deliberately created a pedigree to suit their own stories. It's not hard to figure out the fabrication when the genealogy doesn't fit in any of the Ynys Prydein kingdoms. The argument then goes that Geoffrey's Arthur was a high king, and so this pedigree is of that of the Ynys Prydein. He did this deliberately because he knew Ynys Prydein was not a legitimate governmental setup. As such, there were no records, and so he simply created one.

These kinds of activities get raised numerous times by the various authors like Christopher Gidlow. Because the peripheral information could not be relied upon and people like Geoffrey felt free to simply invent it, the whole subject should be outright dismissed. This line of thinking is simply ridiculous. The reason it is brought up is to limit what would be legitimate references to knowing whether there really was a true King Arthur. In this case, it gets quickly squashed by to Gildas, Bede and Nennius. Quite literally tons of other references are dismissed because of a reoccurring minor mistake at the local Tuath level.

Here is a specific example of the importance of the local annals. One of the earliest recorded event of this description comes with Saint Columba of Iona (Scotland). He received his land grant from King Conal mac Comgaill of Dalriada circa AD 571. King Conal definitely had his own record of the grant. St. Columba, having a shadow record of the charter, guaranteed that the king would not go back on his grant. It was a safety net, so to speak.

Up until the 9th century, you now have an excess of records everywhere, and for historians like Chris Barber, who wrote *King Arthur: The Mystery Unraveled*, things get a bit confusing. Changing political events and records being destroyed cause an excess of duplication. With the coming of the Saxons, the various Briton kingdoms like Cantii and Trinovantes are consumed. Political instability amongst the remaining Briton kingdoms (as was seen with Vortigern) result in kingdoms sacked and renamed (as was the case with Powy and Gwent). In this chaos, people are rewriting as quickly as possible, and a lot of it is simply wrong. When the local monasteries try to do a catch-up on the changing political upheaval, they end up recording things inaccurately. As it is, when the Vikings show up in the early 9th century, the whole system goes to hell in a handbasket.

Of course, the Vikings proved to be the most devastating of them all. When they sacked Lindisfarne, they destroyed everything. This became their signature form of operation as they swept across the British Isles. Iona, Jarrow and Clonmacnoise were sacked. Luckily because of the open-field locality of Clonmacnoise, the destruction wasn't complete; the monks were able to get away with much of their records and valuables. This rescue attempt has an enormous impact on the legend of Arthur as a result. From the Viking Age alone, the records are scattered and broken up. Some kingdoms have annals still intact, others have their chronicles rescued, and in a very few cases, the pedigree, annals and chronicles all still in full operation. This is particularly true in south-east Wales because the Vikings did not penetrate this part of the country.

Around AD 880, Alfred the Great made a mad scramble to rescue much of the Briton records that had not been destroyed. Using only part of the amassed documents, he ordered the creation of what is famously known as the *Anglo-Saxon Chronicles (ASC)*. Scribes were assembled with the purpose of putting together, for the first time, a uniquely Anglo-Saxon past. Other than folklore, the Saxons for the most part did not have records of their own. Because so little of the Briton documents were used in the composition of the ASC, it suffered a uniformity with the Briton chronicles. It is almost a completely an independent document onto itself, even though the two cultures have had a shared history for well over 400 years. For example, there is very little in it that can be lined up with such documents like the *Welsh Triads*. Since its conception, it has caused for centuries a real quandary because much of what is in it cannot be confirmed by documents that predate it. It has naturally split the academic community into two camps; those who accept the Briton chronicles, and those who accept the Anglo-Saxon chronicles. Because the ASC is devoid of any of the typical Celtic bard content, rational scholars prefer it over the Briton records. The problem with this approach is that an entire culture gets overlooked, and valuable information, particularly on King Arthur, is absent. This one move caused an enormous conundrum that is with us to this very day.

It is from Alfred the Great that a simple policy of recognition starts us on our modern way to knowing what is true and what is not. In his time, it was well-established that there were literarily tons of documents about. Sorting through it all was undoubtedly a nightmare when he wanted to compose his famous *Anglo-Saxon Chronicles*. He knew instinctively to go for the documents that were in the various religious and royal centres. Plus, he watched out for the copying done by the neighbouring centres or petty kingdoms. As it is, the scribes put the *Anglo-Saxon Chronicle* together, which is for the most part pretty good. Remarkably, it is one of the most reliable sources for determining British history. However, be aware that much of its sources are from the Welsh. It is from the *Anglo-Saxon Chronicles* that scholars can quickly see the elaborate embellishment Geoffrey did in his *Historium*.

This next part has a pivotal impact on this whole subject of documents, and that is Henry VIII's famous reformation in 1534. A powerful political upheaval gripped the country in Henry's determination to marry Anne Boleyn. The Act of Supremacy is where he wrenches all papal authority for himself. Well aware that the spiritual authorities in Canterbury would oppose him, he has the trusted Thomas Cromwell devise a penalty document, so to speak, called the *Praemunire*. This document gave the Crown the authority in which to impose a financial penalty and tax on the Church. To ensure the Church could pay, Cromwell went across the country to see the methods of raising funds through religious feasts and property value of the monasteries. It turned out it was excessive. In what has become known as the Dissolution of the Monasteries, Cromwell had his officials sweep through the country and ransack all the monasteries of their wealth, particularly their ancient literature. The books and documents were haphazardly thrown into the Tower.

To say this caused an enormous mishmash of historical records is an understatement. Rightly so, critics say you can no longer rely on the past records because now they don't know where they came from, and they are definitely no longer in order. Therefore, everything I have said on the probable grounds for unreliability through a standard miscommunication has just been amplified to the nth degree. The Harleian MS 3859 document on King Arthur is claimed to be a powerful example of the Reformation. This book was compiled from all the loose-end documents found in the Tower, and the compilation was not done with any degree of accuracy. As it is, those who refer to this source are called into question immediately.

The compiling of the Harleian MS 3859 that largely represents Wales's overall royal genealogies was done in a haphazard manner. The document has been dated to AD 988. As such, the sequence of events and dates are seriously questioned. The attention it draws to itself is the genealogy of Glywysing, starting with King Tewdrig circa AD 410. Here is the first official reference at a national level to King Arthur, and the dates fit perfectly to the time frame around the Battle of Badon. Because the entire composition is admittedly slapped together, experts feel they can disregard it and concentrate primarily on Gildas and Nennius. Perhaps the real reason why scholars are staying away from the Harleian MS 3859 is because even in its chaotic condition, it largely agrees with the *Llandaff Charter* at Cathedral Church of Llandaff. This document managed to survive the Reformation intact, and it was ascertained by experts that the dates of people and events in it were accurate. Needless to say, it has the first serious major corroboration on the real existence of the legendary King Arthur. The last thing anyone was expecting to happen from the Reformation was a revelation to the true identity of one of Britain's greatest personalities. This is the kind of thing that often happens in archaeology: a potential disaster takes place, and from it a remarkable discovery is uncovered.

This discovery verifies that Arthur is without question from Wales, and his exact identity can be quickly disclosed. Further pursuit of the inexhaustible opinions on the relevancy to the authenticity of the documents is now nothing more than an issue of conceptual semantics.

The truth is like a lion.
You don't have to defend it.
Let it loose.
It will defend itself.

—St. Augustine

6

Arthur ap Muerig Dilemma

When the glass breaks
Over the well
Tears do follow it
Down into the swell.

Though small the pieces be,
The clarity of the
Moment is beyond
The measure of a sea

Try not to cut yourself in your sorrow
When searching for the water loss,
For it will be
Forgotten by sunset tomorrow.

—"The Glass Well," 17th-century Welsh poem

Let's return to where we last left off, with Ambrosius Aurelianus watching Ynys Emrys burning to the ground (with Vortigern inside it). No one mourns the death of Vortigern because he was a tyrant, and people were happy to see Ambrosius return from exile. Ambrosius was spoken of kindly by everyone, especially by Bede and Nennius. It turns out he ends up being quite the hero of Dark Ages Briton. Ambrosius is identified by Bede as being a former Roman Briton of the purple robe. This means his genealogy comes from a

Roman emperor line. What emperor it may have been, we are never told. All we do know of the man is he did well against the Saxons.

After the Saxons had assassinated the Briton princes on Salisbury Plains, they were confident they could take the country with very little difficulty. Following the exploits of Ambrosius, it would appear the Saxons came in force over a number of years, starting in AD 460 and going through to AD 475. We do not know how many assaults were made, but the impression (especially by Bede) is that they were numerous. Each one was repulsed.

Historians and archaeologists have verified that the Saxons were contained in the south-east corner of England for a considerable amount of time. If we use the *Anglo-Saxon Chronicles* for when Cerdic arrived, circa AD 500, it shows that Saxons still only occupied Kent and the southern region of Essex.

On an interesting note, the military successes by Ambrosius are recorded in the *Annals of Ulster*. It adds to his reputation of being a competent leader. By contrast, these records show the Irish, under Ard-Ri Loegaire, conducted a large-scale campaign against the Britons in AD 460, the results of which were not very successful. It was soon after this that King Loegare is no longer the Ard-Ri of Ireland. Officially we do not know what happened to the Ard-Ri, but the suspicion is due to his repeated failures, he was removed as head of the country. If true, the Druids were the ones who have the authority to tell him to step down from the throne. Note that these events happen at the time Ambrosius is the overall king (Pendragon) of the Ynys Prydein confederacy.

Ambrosius's successes had likely the same frustrating effects on the Saxons as it did on the Scotti. However, the Saxons had a Feudal like system, and the kings were more like dictators than anything else. The Saxons realised if they could not defeat their opponents on the battlefield, they would resort to more devious methods of overcoming their misfortunes, and it again came in the way of an assassin. Whoever this person was, he managed to penetrate the Briton defences and slip into Ambrosius's army camp, likely at Viroconium (Wroxeter). Circa AD 475, Ambrosius was killed by way of poisoning.

From AD 475 to 485, the various chronicles and annals are silent, so no one is sure what came after the assassination. However, via a local bard poem, a King Geraint of Dumnonia appears to have succeeded Ambrosius as the High King of Ynys Prydein. Some authorities are generous in giving the title "Pendragon" to Ambrosius, and so it is fair that the same should be accorded to Geraint.

The poem, which numerous sources say is genuine, tells of a naval assault by the Saxons at Longborth (Plymouth, Cornwall) circa AD 501. The poem clearly states there was an Arthur who helped the king fight off the invaders. This Arthur is fully credited as being the legendary King Arthur in his younger years. Chris Barber, in *King Arthur: The Mystery Unraveled*, and Christopher Gidlow, in *Revealing King Arthur*, are insistent the reference is about the genuine King Arthur. Jean Markale is the source we have to use to verify that the poem meets the bard Celtic stanza requirements, and they do.

Taking the time to make sure the poem is authentic is crucial to everything that comes after this. It is technically the first time King Arthur's name is mentioned, and from it experts are able to precisely date the legendary king's period. Christopher Gidlow ventures in saying that Gildas actually mentions Arthur first, but using the meaning of the name "Bear" (of all the land). However, because he used the term in a verse format, it became interpreted as artistic license. This is another academic complication to fathom, but we shall simply accept the poem and move on.

Now that the name is at last mentioned and it is in the correct time frame, it cannot be helped that a bit of a scramble has happened of where he came from. From numerous sources, the answer is that no one knows. Even Francis Pryor doesn't want to risk making a guess on the whereabouts. I, on the other hand, don't feel it is that big of an issue. If Arthur was real, chances are he came from somewhere nearby. The Graint poem clearly indicated the Dumnonia king did not have much time to anticipate the Saxon attack. Also, based on Arthur's accomplishments, his status had to have been fairly high. Everyone would agree he was an exceptional warrior. As another example, King Crymthann of Ireland is our proof that in order to be exceptionally talented, you were trained by the very best, like the Fianna warrior elite. However, to be part of this special group, you had to have been born of nobility. This becomes one of our biggest clues. The indications suggest Arthur was of such a status. Looking for a Fionn McCool or a Percival is not the situation this time. Therefore, the two parameters are fully met: Arthur was from nearby and was a person of a high rank, likely a king of some sort.

The poem is about the King of Dumonia, and so the first search should be of King Geraint's pedigree. It turns out there are no Arthurs in his family line. Therefore, we move onto the other surrounding kingdoms from where likely Arthur may have been. Once more, the name Arthur is well-recognized as a Deisi Celtic name. The Deici Celts resided in what was formally the Demetae Celtic nation of south-west Wales, now known as Dyfed. Going through their royal pedigree reveals an Arthur, but his time period is the late 500s. The famous poem "Y Gododdin" managed to grab Geoffrey of Monmouth's attention, where it was clearly stated that the real King Arthur was from Gwynedd (north-west Wales). Unfortunately, we find that Gwynedd is at this time still an extremely young country taken over by the Gododdin King Cunedda. The royal pedigree is very short, and there is no Arthur on the list. Mind you, since I mention Geoffrey of Monmouth, his pedigree of Gwynedd was one of his greatest embellishments ever. Staying in Wales, the next kingdom is Powy, and though it's a sizable country because of Vortigern, its history is also short, as is its pedigree. And of course, there is no Arthur to be found. This cleans up all the non-contenders on the Arthur search.

There are two Briton countries left, and they provide the most exciting results yet. The first one is Rheged. With Rheged, there is an Arthur, and he does meet the correct time period. However, when you look at Christopher Gidlow's research on this Arthur, the man begins to fade from the picture quite quickly. It is not so much him but the country he represents. As must have been figured out when King Coel was its ruler, Rheged had been distracted by the Scotti and the Picts. Their borders had never been secured, and when you go through their history, they had never been involved in any joint venture with the other Briton countries.

The second Briton country and our last hope to find Arthur is Glywysing (Glamorgan). This country takes us for a bit of a ride. At first glance, you are deceived regarding what you are looking at. If you are an impatient reader and simply want the highlights, there is an Arthur here, but like Dyfed he was in the wrong century. He is registered in the late 6th century—obviously too late. However, by taking an extra minute to read some of the small print on this Arthur, you come across an interesting statement, like in Wikipedia, where it states he is the son of King Muerig. It then goes to say "claimed" to be possibly the Legend King Arthur. At once, this becomes puzzling when you see the dates do not line up at all. Why would they say this when it doesn't make sense? King Arthur is precisely dated from AD 475 to 539. This was figured out in part because of the Geraint poem. Thus there is no mistaking what we are looking for. From the innocuous statement, our curiosity is at once struck. Thus we have to look into this just a little bit further.

The next thing, though equally innocent, does draw even more attention to this Glywysing Arthur. Official historical sources, both American and British, are very matter-of-fact in saying that this Arthur had a sister named Anna. It is no big deal at first. So the man has a sister—so what? It turns out Anna is a major key to a series of confusing dates. She gives birth to a boy who becomes the famous Saint Samson. Saint Samson is heavily recorded in Church records as a real and great historical figure in Welsh history. Because he has been canonized, there is no question of his authenticity. In fact, they have a document he signed in Paris as part of a church accord in AD 556. As soon as you see that, there is something obviously wrong here. How could he have signed this document when he wasn't even born yet? This would clearly be the case if Arthur of Glywysing was supposedly his uncle.

If that little bit of confusion grabs your attention, then this next part will really be interesting. The Glywysing pedigree is written with no special emphasis made on anything. It is claimed King Meurig is Arthur's father and lived in the mid-6th century. That makes perfect sense. Meurig's father was King Tewdrig, and he lived in the early 5th century. In fact, one source says he was a young boy when the Romans left the island. This statement throws you in for a bit of bewilderment. How can that be so? Time-wise, it makes no sense at all. If this was the case, Tewdrig would be well over 100 years old, or his son Meurig is over 100 years old. In those days, the average life expectancy was only 40 years. This is a typo, or clearly someone does not have the facts straight. Because the confusion exists on either side of this Arthur, it would seem to me the dates on this man are incorrect. Because Saint Samson is the most solid historical figure in this whole equation, it's not hard to adjust. Go back one generation with Anna (Samson's mother) and place Arthur and Meurig in the 5th century and not the 6th. Then it all lines up perfectly. Tewdrig is early 5th century, Meurig is mid-5th century and Arthur is late 5th century. Add in the fact Glywysing sat right next door to Dumonia, and so this Arthur is more than likely to have come to the aid of King Geraint. Suddenly the Geraint poem is completely credible.

Chris Barber, in his book *King Arthur: The Mystery Unraveled,* takes a tour of the churches around south-east Wales, particularly at Llandwitt, to verify that the Arthur of Meurig actually lived in the late 5th century and not the 6th, as it is officially stated. Once more, when it came to the churches, they went to great care in recording as much of the events around them as possible. For example, when a king gave a religious order for a grant of land to build a church on, it was recorded in the margin of their gospels; it acted as a deed. Sure enough, Chris found that there were several churches in the region that had such recordings. Many were found to have King Arthur's name in them, and the dates were all the late 5th century. Because there are no records with Arthur's name in a later date, it would be at least one confirmation that King Arthur of Glamorgan living in the late 6th century is wrong. The Internet referencing data system appears to not be very accurate.

The question is how such a gross error of dates to a local king could have happened. British (and to a larger extent American) historians are more than satisfied to believe the real King Arthur never existed and was strictly an illusion. In this line of thinking, who cares about a king in the small province of Glamorgan? If it is believed this Arthur is not the legendary King Arthur, then clean up the mistake. What difference will it make in the long run? Yet I have found from a variety of different conventional sources that there is an insistence to keep the mistake on the books; even Wikipedia has it incorrect.

I could go down the conspiracy road, from which no doubt I would have a lot of support from Alan Wilson, and say it is an intentional mistake. Having a real historical Arthur figure would have an enormous impact on the overwhelming, fabricated mystery that has developed over the centuries. However, I am going to stay with the argument that it is more likely an issue of carelessness. The Arthur mystery was developed as a result of historical events (like the Reformation) disrupting the records on a real person, resulting in having him misplaced. Remember that we are talking about the Dark Ages of wolfskins and wicker huts, not the glamorous medieval age of knights in shining armour. As such, it should not be that big of a deal to sort out this insignificant local mismatch.

The reason I take a less controversial position of people being misdated is because events like the Vikings, the Norman invasion and the Reformation did have an impact, causing a great deal of confusion. According to Christopher Gidlow, the Harleian MS 3859 is currently in British hands, possibly in the National Archives of London. Gidlow's research has led him to believe the loose documents were assembled into a book around 1880. Whoever did the compilation was not sure of the order, only that the pages were of Welsh origins. At least we can be satisfied that the editor was aware of this and knew the pages were of royal pedigrees. Personally, I am not in tune to know that there would be a sequential order for the subject, but apparently Welsh authorities say there is. Because they are not in order, it would clearly show the British antiquity authorities are not familiar with it either. Despite all this confusion, the fact is there is one page in the Harleian that draws everybody's attention, and that is the pedigree of Glamorgan. This pedigree has a confirmation lineup of the three kings Tewdrig, Muerig and Arthur. Thus at the national British level, the Welsh local records are verified, making Wikipedia references superfluous. The Arthur of Glamorgan is, by official, national and provincial records, squarely dated to the late 5th century. Because he is the only one found in this time frame, it is reasonable to believe he is the famous King Arthur who has been lost to history.

Personally, I'm satisfied that this man from Glywysing (Glamorgan) is a suitable candidate to be the genuine King Arthur. The status and the corrected dates meet the requirements of the Welsh legend. The thing to remember here is the legendary King Arthur by Geoffrey of Monmouth was a huge embellishment placed in the romantic chivalric age of the Great Crusades. Far too many people have bought into the nonsense, and that is whom they are chancing after. Such a person does not exist. The real King Arthur lived in a very different world, where everyone lived in filthy palisade fortresses, sanitation was dreadful, food was limited, disease was rampant and a king was more a warlord than anything. He certainly did not sit on a throne or live in a palace. If you were not good with a sword your chances of survival were not very high. Our King Arthur is rough-looking, likely wears a wolf skin, eats with his hands, hasn't washed in at least a month, is illiterate, has taken dozens of women to bed, gets into fights all the time and has personally killed hundreds of men. This is the kind of person who would fit the times and command a lot of respect from the rough soldiers all around him. This kind of King Arthur is not hard for anyone to accept, and thus he's not particularly hard to find either. When you read Bede's description of everyone of the time, particularly Maelgwyn of Gwenydd, anyone could have been King Arthur. All the petty kings of Wales were tyrants and, other than Ambrosius, none had any redeeming qualities. In this light, the real King Arthur was simply a skilled, bloodthirsty murderer. Whether he came from Glamorgan or Powy, who really cares? The bottom line is you did not want to mess with this man.

Technically, I could stop here. As far as I am concerned, Arthur ap Meudrig is the most likely candidate to represent the legendary Arthur of Camelot. However, I know if I don't at least comment on Arturo Mac Aedan of Dalriada, the fans of Simon Andrew Stirling's book *The King Arthur Conspiracy* will have a lot say. It is a fact that many of the embellishments in Geoffrey's writing came from this Artur, notably Guinevere as his wife and the great magician Merlin. Merlin was fabricated from a real person known as Merddin Wylit, who was an insane prince going around and telling prophecies. Stirling feels that from these few points, the real King Arthur was from Scotland and not from Wales.

Artur Mac Aedan was the son of the great warrior King Aedan Mac Gabrian, who reigned Dalriada from AD 573 to 603. From the *Annals of Ulster,* Aedan was a very colourful leader and gave the Scotiis their second big chance in regaining the glories of Niall of the Nine Hostages. There is almost no mention of Artur for the simple reason it was Aedan who was capturing all the glory. Artur was a capable commander under his father's guidance, but at no time did he stand out on his own, Aedan even gets mentioned by Adonman of the Iona monastery as a generous king. For both Ireland and its province Dalriada, it was an extraordinary time.

Aedan Mac Gabrian burst out of Dalriada circa AD 374 and attacked the Picts. The famous King Bridei, who was Christianized by Saint Columba, ruled the Picts. He had nowhere near the fighting skills of his predecessor, Drest of a Hundred Battles. As it was, the entire west coast of Pictland (Scotland) fell into Scotii hands. This is all credited to Aedan's brilliant field tactics. Unfortunately, Artur is credited with almost nothing. Circa AD 585, Aedan and his newly renovated navy took the Orkney Islands. At this point, the Picts were in real danger of being completely encircled by the Scotii. Luckily, Aedan suddenly had an unexplained change of plans.

Around AD 390, Aedan struck deep into Northern Gododdin and took it over after a bloody fight with the Miathi (Maeatae) Picts and the Votadinii Celts. These two groups are recorded as serious problems to Roman rule. Again, the victories are all given to Aedan.

Then as the 7th century turned, Aedan again strikes, this time straight south into what was now the kingdom of Alt Clut (Strathclyde). There isn't much written on this, but Aedan went up against the suborn Novantii Celts in this conquest. Again, upon reading up on this campaign, there is no mention of Artur, his son.

Circa AD 605, an unexpected change of events happens. The Anglo King Aethelfrith of Bernicia marches into southern Gododdin and defeats Mynyddog Mwynfawr, from which the famous poem *Y Gododdin* is written. Simon Stirling feels that the King Arthur mentioned in the poem is referring to the legendary King Arthur, not Artur mac Aedan. This invasion by the Anglos enrages Aedan as a personal insult. Where does Aethelfrith get off challenging his authority in the region? Bernicia was at the time a very small Anglo kingdom, so in reality it was a bold move on Aethelfrith's part. As it is, without thinking Aedan quickly marches an army into southern Gododdin to confront the Angles. It turns into a disaster, and the Scotii are routed. It is in this turn of events that Artur is killed. The Scotii are driven all the way back to Dalriada. In the Scotti calamity, Breidi takes full advantage of it and retakes the Picts lands on the west coast. In the nick of time, the Ard-Ri Aed Allan of Ireland steps in and prevents Aethelfrith from making it a complete sweep by taking Dalriada. Though Ireland had been seriously reduced in size from its glory days of Niall, it was still the most powerful country of the British Isles.

It comes as no surprise that King Aedan quickly disappeared from history, as too did his son Artur.

From the official historical accounts, Artur Mac Aedan is badly overshadowed by his father, and he hardly makes for a great legend. From here, it is all too easy to dismiss this Arthur from being the legendary king. From the very start of the official time period to the legendary Arthur, Artur is too late. Second, this Arthur never takes on the Saxons, as both Bede and Nennius are insistent upon. Next, Artur is too far away to help King Geraint of Dumonia. Even if it were possible, Dumonia was one of the countries the Irish were raiding. Artur would hardly find himself helping the Britons against the Saxons. Lastly—and this is the really big point that will be addressed in the next chapter—is the Battle Badon. This is a monumental event dated in stone as happening in AD 515. There was no Badon-like battle that happened in Gododdin or in Pictland at the time of Artur and which all the Scribes of the British Isles wrote about, as they did in the area of Bath (Nennius). On these points, Artur is eliminated from possibility.

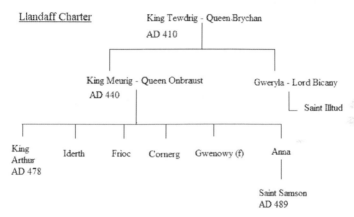

"King Arthur's Pedigree"

7

Arthur's Campaign and Badon/Baedan

Knights, the gift of freedom is yours by right
But the home we seek resides not in some distant land,
It's in us, and in our actions this day!
If this be our destiny, then so be it.
But let history remember.
That as free men,
We chose to make it so.

—Arthur, from *King Arthur* (2004)

If there is one event that is the defining moment to the identity of King Arthur, it is the battle of Badon (or Baedon) as described by Nennius. There are some historians, but not very many, who claim that it was Ambrosius who fought at this battle. However, the Anglo-Saxons outright dismiss this possibility because they made sure he was dead in AD 475. Further, from a variety of Welsh annals, they have this man born in AD 401, and thus he would have been 114 years old had he actually fought at this battle. When you consider the average age in this time was 35 years, it would have been impossible for Ambrosius to have been there.

As far as the scribes of Briton, Amorica, Pictland and Scotti (Ireland) were concerned, Badon was a major historical event equal to D-Day. The battle was noted in dozens of annals and chronicles throughout the islands. Those records that mention the name of the Briton who fought the battle agree with Nennius that an Arthur is the one who was there. Where the battle took place is still in contention. A majority of historians believe it happened near the Roman civita Aquae Sulis or Bath (Somerset). With everything I have read on it, particularly with the *Anglo-Saxon Chronicles,* I am leaning this way as well. However, a close second would be Mynydd Baedan, 10 kilometres west of Cardiff. What gives this second site credit is the fact the Saxons had conducted naval attacks on both Wales and Cornwall before. Unfortunately, there is no archaeological evidence to support this. There is evidence that the Saxons did reach Somerset via the Thames River. The two locations are very close to each other, and therefore Arthur ap Meudrig is still the best fit.

Nennius is the only one who describes the events leading up to Badon. In summary, it took Arthur about 10 years (circa AD 505–515) to lead the kings of Ynys Prydein in a series of battles around northern Briton that ended at Badon. British historians have gone to great lengths over the last 200 years to decipher the real route, or whether in fact Nennius simply made it all up. Once more I have found historians in general have annualized this subject to death, working the whole time inside a bubble. With this criteria, they accept without reservation that Arthur was fighting the Saxons the whole way through. However, once you look outside the bubble of what was really going on in Briton, you quickly realise there were no Saxons at all to speak of, except for at Badon. The reality of the situation was that from Rheged all the way to Dalriada, the area was occupied by the Picts and Scots. According to Nennius, Arthur started his campaign by marching north and then he came south at the end.

By now, it should be clear that post-Roman Briton was in a dilemma of being encircled by enemies on three fronts. On the west at this time, they were, for the most part, under Irish/Scot control. They had lost much of their former momentum of conquest, and so they were back to raiding. In the north-east were the Picts. They had just been pushed out of Norfolk by the Anglos but still had a firm grip of everything north of Lincoln, all the way to Gododdin. The Saxons were just beginning to break out of Kent under a new and aggressive leader known as Cerdic. North of the Thames and moving in a north-westerly direction were the Anglos under a vicious leader known as Ælle (pronounced "Eye-Ella"). He was making the best progress of all the foreign invaders. These are the hard archaeological facts that have been serious researched by Francis Pryor. The one thing that can be dismissed from Nennius's account is Arthur fighting against solely the Saxons. That was not the case at all.

Where we should start this part of the story is with the arrival of the Saxon warlord Cerdic and his son Cynric. In AD 508, they landed on the western shores of Kent in three warrior ships. According to the ASC, Cerdic is a fearsome and determine leader who in no time at all gets the local Saxons to join him in a campaign against the Britons. For the next 7 years, it says, he slugs it out with his opponents. Progress was painfully slow, and it isn't till AD 518 that he finally makes it to the Island of Wight. Still, Cerdic isn't the type to give up. The ASC clearly states he is driving west non-stop. There is no record of his casualties, but when you consider he was fighting hard for 7 years, it must have been horrible. It is interesting that for the years AD 515–518, the chronicles are silent of his activities. The ASC was routinely silent when it came to any victory the Britons had achieved. It gives the strong indication that in those three years, the Britons had the upper hand, and it also alludes that Badon did in fact happen.

Then there is the Anglo warlord Ælle. The chronicles don't say where he started, only that he has crossed the Thames and is heading for Salisbury Plains. Historians are in the general agreement that he makes it to the edge by AD 515. What is made clear is Ælle is not interested in any alliances with the Saxons. However, as always scholars debate this on account that Badon was a major battle that lasted for three days, if we are to believe Nennius. Cerdic didn't have that large of a force to have fought the battle himself, and therefore everything points to the fact that he must have had an alliance with the Angles. Further, scholars and archaeologists are in agreement that after the battle, the territories of both the Angles and the Saxons shrank in size. That gives additional support that there was likely some form of alliance. Now, if we are to carry on with this line of thinking, a naval operation is out of the question. The Anglos were too far inland to have suddenly turned around and joined the Saxons in a naval assault. Further, from what is written about Cerdic, he himself did not have enough ships to have pulled it off. To this date, archaeologists say the evidence of a large Saxon fleet like the Irish had is near non-existent. I believe that under these circumstances, the assault on Badon was a land assault, and Bath was the likely target. If we accept that it was land campaign Arthur conducted, as Nennius claims, it becomes yet another reason why a naval assault was not likely. The Anglo-Saxon flank would have been exposed to attack, and the evidence supports Cerdic and Ælle would not have risked it.

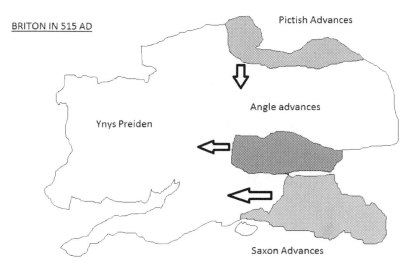

"Directions of Invaders to Briton"

From here, we travel north-east, starting on the northern shores of modern Norfolk and then moving all the way up to Inverness in the heart of Pictland. This stretch of land was under the control of the Picts. Archaeologists today are able to know this, but such people did not exist in the time of Nennius and Bede; they were completely dependent on what was found in their own small libraries. In the *Historium*, Nennius was convinced that in AD 501, Northumbria in particular was under Saxon control. The truth is they never made it that far. It was the Angles who were marching north, not the Saxons. Neither Nennius nor Bede knew the difference. Gildas knew but simply wouldn't comment on it; he was more concerned about writing up his religious diatribe than reflecting real history.

Anyway, the Picts were under the reign of yet another Drest (II). Like the former (Drest of a Hundred Battles), he was ambitious to expand the Pictish empire. The Picts controlled more of Briton than the Irish or the Anglo-Saxons put together. At this time, the most incredible site in all of Pictland was the Burghead Fortress. This place was about 30 kilometres east of Inverness on the coastline. It was the main naval port for the vast fleet of ships the Picts had. According to one scribe from Jarrow (Northumbria), around AD 500, 200 ships at this establishment were destroyed due to a thunderstorm. A second account came in the 11th century: a scribe from Northumbria wrote that when Burghead was attacked by the Vikings, it took them a whole week to overtake the megafortress. From these two accounts alone, there is no doubt this place was massive, and it surely supports what the *Cambria Annals* is saying about large naval attacks by the Picts down the East Coast.

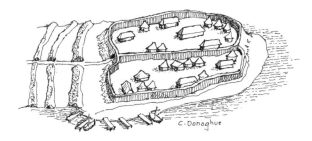

"Burghead Fortress"

There is very little known about Pictish ships, and so perhaps a moment should be taken in describing them. The Pictish navy comprised of over 300 miniature versions of Viking-designed ships. The *Pictish Chronicles* in Glascow give a detail account of the ship's crew. The numbers help in getting an idea of the size. Each ship had a crew of 27 sailors and soldiers. There was one mask and eight sets of oars, four on each side. A Viking ship is said had an average crew of 37, with 26 oars (13 on each size). The average length of the ship was 54 feet. If we use the Scandinavian crew size as a measuring stick, we can estimate how long a Pictish ship may have been. It likely worked out to this 39 feet. That is a plausible size. Also, the ships were built better than their Irish counterparts because they did not need animal hides for water sealant. If indeed the ships were 39 feet long, that is a big enough craft to safely sail the seas. From the research I did on my book *The Picts of Scotland,* I discovered the Picts had a fairly busy trade with the Saxons in Denmark during the time of the Romans. Travelling from Scotland to Denmark is a considerable distance, and so the ships had to have been sturdy.

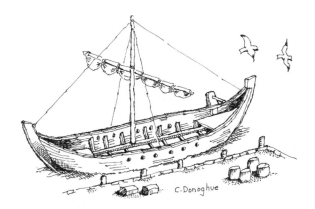

"Typical Pictish Cargo Ship"

There are no written records of Drest II ever having an encounter with the Britons, but archaeologists have confirmed his reign marked the peak of Pictish expansion. After Drest II, the boarders of Pictland dramatically imploded. It is yet another piece of evidence that the timing is interesting. The Saxon advance was halted, and so too was the Pictish advance. It gives credence to the claim that what Nennius said of Arthur's pre-Badon campaign is believable.

Going from Inverness directly west is Dunadd, the capital of the Dalriada, the provincial kingdom of Ireland. Here is the heart of the Scotii stronghold. As mentioned before, the people of Dalriada and Ulster still referred to themselves as Scots, not Irish, as the trend was taking over the mainland.

The Tuathe king of Dalriada at this time was a man by the name of Fergus Mor. He was slightly ambitious but preferred to keep things stable. He wanted his tax base improved while on the throne, and so according to the *Tigernach,* in AD 501 he stretched his borders into Ult Clut. By modern standards, Dalriada occupied all of Argyle and Strathclyde. The Scotti advance does not go any further than this until King Aedan comes to the throne.

The Ard-Ri of Ireland itself was Domangart Reti, and he reigned from AD 505–510. It wasn't very long, but he developed a very good rapport with the Celtic Christian Church. Apparently, he was very generous in providing financial assistance to the Church. Under his rule, Bangor, Armagh and Clonmacnoise prospered. Briefly, the Celtic Christian Church had its origins in Ireland and spread into

Scotland and finally Northumbria. It had no connections with the Roman Catholic Church until after the Synod of Whitby in AD 664.

The *Annals of Cambria* state that the Irish incursion was still going on in the early 6th century. Even though Domangart Reti was focused on the development of the Celtic Church, his ships were still ravaging the western coastlines of Briton. According to Alice S. Green in *History of the Irish State to 1014,* the Irish economy was doing exceptionally well from AD 400 onwards. She claims there was a lot of innovation going on in agriculture, though she will not credit the fact that it may have been the result of the monasteries; I believe it was. The monks brought to Ireland from mainland Europe technology that wasn't there before. When Ard-Ri Eochaid was High King circa AD 375, the Irish economy centred on cattle, exporting metals like tin and gold and the slave trade. That was practically all gone by the time the monastic movement was established. Agriculture was still the mainstay, but there were some major refinements in the process in that mills began to appear. As it was, the volume of food dramatically increased, where they could now export the surplus.

One last addition to all this is was what was going on in Europe, particularly in Gaul (France). Between AD 470 and 511 a powerful man named Clovis of the Franks was sweeping away the last remnants of Roman rule. He was undoubtedly a very skilful warrior. Legend has it that King Arthur fought Clovis (Monmouth and Malory), but the truth is it's not likely. Had Arthur in fact faced Clovis, the scribes in Gaul would have definitely noted it. However, there are no recordings by any legitimate sources to say any British king ever set foot in Gaul. In Brittany, there are a dozen or so "legendary" accounts of Arthur being there, but that is it. The annals and the chronicles are completely silent on this subject. Alan Wilson feels Geoffrey of Monmouth may have gotten confused with the Roman Arthur (in Gaul) of the Magnus Maximus period and "accidently" placed it in the wrong century. Personally, knowing Geoffrey, I think he did it deliberately.

Thus for the first time, you have now have broader account of what was going all around the Britons at the time when Arthur was elected as Dux Bullorum. From the real evidence, it would seem that the threat to the Britons was not the Anglos or the Saxons, as Bede and Nennius would have you believe, but in fact the Picts. They were sweeping down the East Coast and had renewed their friendship with the Saxons, as they had under Drest of Hundred Battles; there was no stopping them. During the Roman occupation, the Picts had a long trade relationship with the Saxons that is only recorded in *The Pictish Chronicles* and nowhere else. Only during the Vortigern years was it interrupted. Next were the Irish. There is no doubt their sudden takeover of Ult Clut must of made people very nervous, in that there may be the return of another Niall in the guise of Domangart Reti. In summary, the fact is the threat from the north was very real. Briton was indeed at a crossroads, and the evidence does support that the Britons had to act soon or face extinction. Now, when we look at Nennius's 12-battle campaign of Arthur prior to the Battle of Badon, it all makes sense.

Arthur's 12-Battle Campaign

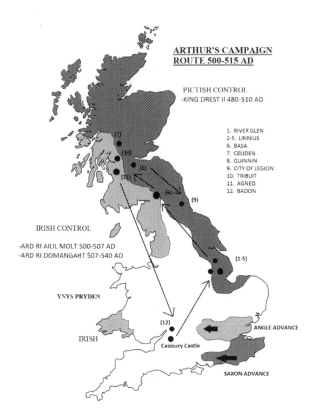

ARTHUR'S CAMPAIGN
ROUTE 500-515 AD

PICTISH CONTROL
-KING DREST II 480-510 AD

1. RIVER GLEN
2-5. LINNIUS
6. BASA
7. CELIDEN
8. GUINNIN
9. CITY OF LEGION
10. TRIBUIT
11. AGNED
12. BADON

IRISH CONTROL

-ARD RI AILIL MOLT 500-507 AD
-ARD RI DOMANGART 507-540 AD

(1-5)

YNYS PRYDEN

(12)

IRISH

ANGLE ADVANCE

Cadbury Castle

SAXON ADVANCE

Again, Nennius is our only source to Arthur's campaign route. It's no secret that there is not much to go on in his description, and because of that, there is a lot criticism regarding him fabricating it. The campaign does have validity because clearly the Saxons were not the only threat to the Britons. In this section, I use the research of three conventional historians like Mike Ashley (*King Arthur*) and two fictional writers, Jack Whyte (*A Dream of Eagles*) and Bernard Cornwell (*Excalibur*). The fictional writers provide an atmospheric twist, revealing a human factor that is not commonly seen in the straight historical literature. What has to be understood from this part is what is believable. Historians in general have examined this portion of the story at face value and inside a glass house. From this kind of perspective, a lot of things don't make any sense. For example, we have established that the Saxons and the Angles in AD 500 were confined to south-east Briton. When Nennius claims Arthur fought the Saxons near Lincoln, that simply isn't true. Thus, a little artistic help is needed to create a more realistic scenario regarding what may have happened. If Arthur didn't fight the Saxons, who did fight, and how did he do it? To answer these questions, we need the assistance of some fictional writers.

Generally speaking, historians accept Nennius's claim that Arthur marched an army all the way to Pictland and Dalriada and back down to Bath Sussex in roughly a 10-year period. He fought a total of 12 battles in this time frame, with Badon being the last. Badon is the only one confirmed as a true historical event. Because historians have verified many of the locations to the 12 battle sites, it would appear they are likely true as well. Because it is a fact that the Saxons and the Angles were restricted to the south, then it has to be Arthur was fighting the Irish and the Picts. The Irish and Pictish chronicles verify that they were encroaching on Briton and that if the Britons did not come out to fight the Celtic invaders, they would have taken the country. That is a certainty. On that principle, Nennius's campaign account is believable.

Using the research from Mike Ashley, Christopher Gidlow and Rodney Castleden, we can put a composite of Arthur's army together. First, Nennius tells us that several of the kings and princes of Yny's Prydein accompanied him on the campaign. No doubt with the lords being present, the supply wagons were extra lengthy, likely carrying their wine urns from Tintagel. Francis Bacon says Tintagel was still in full operation as a trading centre down in Dumnonia at this time. Next, the actual army Arthur is said to have had comprised of 800 cavalry and 5,000 infantry. Castleden is the only one who is convinced Arthur's army was wholly made up of cavalry and nothing else. This doesn't make sense when we get into the deep forests of Calidonia. Cavalry do not fare well in thick forests. If we go with the infantry and cavalry concept, we can believe it was a long campaign involving thousands of soldiers, hundreds of wagons and thousands of miles to cover more than a decade of fighting. This scenario nicely fills in the blanks that are not present in Nennius's account. Again, not to belabour the point, but Nennius was an ardent monk, not a soldier.

He couldn't care less of the practicalities that were involved with a large military force.

Nennius states that the first five battles happened in the Lincoln County region of Briton. Assuming this is accurate, we are in Pict controlled territory. According to the Roman Tacitus, in AD 71 the Picts either fought as a mob when completely confident or by guerrilla style when not so sure. The average Pictish army was recorded to be more than 40,000 men—a size that could easily overwhelm Arthur's force. Therefore it is no doubt he needed cunning to beat the Picts. The *Welsh Chronicles* clearly state Arthur inherited his father's and grandfather's tactical skills. Thus the evidence points to the fact that Arthur was a capable field commander. Because he is credited with winning all five battles, it would validate what the chronicles say about him.

Lincoln County was very close to the region of where the Angles were fighting, and as such it becomes a natural curiosity: How did the two armies not cross paths? The answer is simple. Ælle was too busy fighting the Rheged armies, and he was no friend of the Picts. Had he risked changing direction north, he may have faced three armies (Rheged, Briton and Picts) instead of one. He was having a hard enough time fighting just one army, and so there is no way he would risk taking on two or more. This was probably a point that even Arthur was aware of as he continued moving north after Lincoln.

Many British historians have not included the Celtic infrastructure in the Arthur story, and so defining his role in the campaign is puzzling. It is on this point that there has been enormous debate regarding his title as Dux Bellorum. Was he a king, as is clearly pointed out in the *Llandaff Charter,* or was he a simple warrior and nothing more? The confusion is because most historians will not call the Britons Celts. However, once you do call them Celts, it's not hard to figure out. One has to simply look at such people like Vercingetorix of Gaul and Boudica of the Icenii. Both were local rulers and national commanders at the same time. This is the key, and it verifies quickly that Arthur can be a king and a Dux Bellorum simultaneously. The Celts nominated their joint party war chief in much the same way as the elected their Tuath kings. In the Celtic world of democracy, it is a very natural process that is done very quickly. The kings know from the outset that there will be squabbling if they do not have a central leader to command the combined forces, and so they quickly elect a Dux Bellorum. When the fighting is over, the position is quickly dissolved. As a Celt, Arthur was well aware of this fact. Why it has been such an exhausting discussion for so long is simply because the Anglo-Saxon definition of a king is what's being applied. You can't be a general and a monarch at the same time; you are either one or the other. So very true! But as you can see, that does not hold true in the Celtic culture. Kings were never considered regal. If they screwed up, they were quickly replaced by the Arch-Druid. As such, for men like Corodicus, Vercingetorix and Boudica, having several hats of office was the way the Celts did things, and that is the end of the discussion.

The next debate—and a valid one at that—is, Where did this combined army from the 4 Ynys Prydein kingdoms assemble? I figure the confederacy comprised of Glywysing, Powy, Gwynedd and Dumnonia. The reason I don't include Demetae is because it was part of Ireland, and attacking the Scotti would not have gone over well with the Irish king. This of course brings up the famous subject of Camelot. Did the dreamy castle that Geoffrey described actually exist? He says it was the Roman garrison of Caerleon. The problem with this location is it is too small. The Roman garrison was only capable of holding 4,000 legionnaires and that is it. Arthur had an army of more than 5,000, so he needed a much bigger place to assemble. An archaeological dig that happened at Cadbury Castle in the late 1970s convinced most authorities Camelot was in fact there. This was an enormous Celtic fortress that could house an army of well more than 10,000 men, plus supplies. It sat in between Wales and Cornwall, and so it was ideally situated. I go into this in more detail later.

Now that we have an idea of Arthur's army, we can continue with Nennius's campaign route. It is interesting that the actual battle sites were confirmed through language experts. It turns out that except for a few locations, the routes go in a straight line out and back again. Not to be surprised, I have once more added a little common sense to the march. If you have ever served in the military, you know moving a large force cannot be done on short notice. Further, the Battle of Hastings in 1066 is the classic example of what happens when you race an exhausted army into battle after a long march, like Harold Godwinson did. The results were disastrous. Arthur was far more successful than Harold, and so I would say he kept his army in a straight route and made sure they were fresh for every fight.

Here are some of the specifics. The first place of battle by Nennius is called the Glen. Historians feel there were two locations for this spot. The first one was in Lincoln, near the Humber, and the second one was up by Hadrian's Wall. I quickly dismiss the second place on account of where the next 3 battles take place, in Linius. Linius has been determined as Lincoln, or better still Lincolnshire County. Nennius says Arthur fought the Saxons here. As we know, this is not correct. Other sources claim Arthur fought Octo son Hengist here. This too is incorrect because the timeline does not line up. This is people taking a stab in the dark because they have not taken the time to look at anything other than what Nennius wrote.

The fifth battle was called Dubglas. Dubglas means "black water." I'm not sure why it was centred out by Nennius, because the battle was said also to be in the Linius region.

The sixth battle was at a place called Bassa. The location of this place has been designated to be on the border of Alt Clut and Rheged, near the western coastline. Gidlow is satisfied this is location is accurate. However, Ashley feels it was in Scotland, inland of the Firth of Forth. In either case, Arthur is now taking on the Scots, and the person he is facing is definitely Fergus Mor. As we recall, Fergus Mor had just recently annexed Ult Clut into Dalriada, and so it's reasonable to believe he is now going to defend his newest acquisition.

At this point, we have to take another pause and examine how Arthur was doing it. Nennius fully claims Arthur and his Ynys Prydein kings were successful in all their battles up till now. Here is where we have to use a little fictional writing to help us with the imagination. I found Bernard Cornwall, in *Excalibur,* provides us with the best scenario of how Arthur was doing it. Cornwall appears have studied the real story of Arthur and recognized that he did have a much smaller force then his enemy's. As Tacitus claims, the Picts could marshal a huge army of well more than 20,000 warriors. Such an army could easily smash a small force of 6,000 rough in an open battle. When you consider how large the territory the Picts had in the early 6th century, marshalling such a force is very feasible. At the get-go, Arthur was at a serious disadvantage. Cornwall figured that the only way Arthur could have managed under such difficult conditions was by means of ambush. Arthur would set up his infantry in a restricted, funnel-like ground and then send out his cavalry to draw the enemy into this funnel. Once inside, his infantry would pounce. It is reasonable that he did this because it is exactly what Arminius did to Varus in Germany in the Teutoburg Forest (AD 9).

The seventh battle was named Celidon. Celidon is unanimously agreed to mean Caledonia. The location has been estimated to be on the east side of Scotland, near the Firth of Forth. If so, we are in Meaetae Pict territory. The Meaetae proved to be a devastating force against Agricola in AD 72. Arthur did not have two legions at his disposal, as the Romans did, and so it becomes curious how he fared against such enormous odds in the thick forests of Caledonia. Here, historical fiction writer Jack Whyte (*Uther*) may help us in this regard. The Romans had in their ranks Scythian bowman. They had a short, curved bow that was extremely effective at both long and short range. Perhaps when Ambrosius was in charge of the Briton forces, he implemented this weapon for the Romanization of the Briton forces, and Arthur simply carried on with it. The Meaetae did not have such a weapon, and so they were vulnerable. This would help explain a lot. As we know, Arthur's horses would not have been very effective in a thick forest against huge numbers of Picts. For me, the only way Arthur could have defeated the Picts on their own ground would have been with some sort of special weapon like the bow.

The eighth battle is called Guinnion, said by many to be near Bassa, no doubt taking on the Scots. However, Ashley argues it's a Welsh name, and so that means Arthur would have had to race down to Wales to fight it. I have a problem with this line of thinking. For openers, the ASC makes it clear Cerdic was having a very hard time breaking out of Kent. Therefore, getting into Wales was simply impossible. From that line of reasoning, I am inclined to say Guinnion is somewhere in Northumbria. Again, Nennius fully implies Arthur was successful, and he was likely now fighting the Scots. If true, there seems to be a bit of a theme now to the fighting and that is both the Picts and the Scots are going after Arthur at the same time, or he is going after them at the same time. This scenario is kind of like Napoleon prior to the Battle of Waterloo, where he is desperately trying to keep the British and the Prussians from joining at the Quatre Bras.

The ninth battle is by far the most interesting of them all, and that is at the City of the Legion. All historians I have come across are unanimous that it was at an abandoned Roman garrison of some sort. But what garrison? There were three Roman garrisons that had the reputation of being called a city. The first one was Isca, down in the south-east corner of Wales, near Caerleon. This garrison was the home base, if you will, of the Legio II Augustus. It was big enough to house exactly one full legion, and that was it. Going straight north to the top of Wales, at Chester, was Deva. This garrison was the home base of Legio XX Valeria. Again, the garrison could only house one legion of 4,000 men. Finally, there was Eboracum, up near Hadrian's Wall and on the east side of Briton. This garrison could house 10,000 men at minimum at its peak, and during Severus's campaign in AD 211, it housed up to 20,000 troops. There was no stationary unit here because it was a massive transient base from which units were coming and going all the time. No doubt this was the most impressive fortress of them all. It was the New York City of all the garrison cities on the island. Arthur had already fought tree battles up in the north, and I can't see him racing down to either Isca or Deva to an unlikely chance of fighting the Saxons or the Angles, then racing back and fighting two more battles again against the Picts and the Scots. I am inclined to believe the City of Legion was indeed Eboracum.

The place named Tribuit was where the 10th battle occurred. Tribuit has been claimed to be up near Dunbarton, on the river Clyde. Dunbarton is very close to the Dalriada, capital of Dunadd. The evidence here seems to indicate Arthur was chasing the Scots, and now he wanted to put end to it once and for all. Being that close to Dunadd likely brought out Fergus Mor himself. He probably thought this was enough—time to put down this little upstart in his place. Fergus Mor brought out his full force of around 20,000. Arthur likely knew this and so made an extra effort to thoroughly prepare the ambush. Nennius is so nonchalant about the victory, and so Arthur must have done a great job at it. To know if it was possible that a smaller force in those days could defeat a far greater force of experience, we have another powerful name on this subject, and that is Variatus of the Lusitania rebellion (155–139 BC). They call it the massacre of 148 BC. The location of the battle is not known, but Variatus conducts an ambush in exactly the same fashion as Arminius did at Teutoburgh. The Roman legions were stretched out into a very thin line, and the Lusitanian Celts pounced and slaughtered them all.

After the Battle of Tribuit, there are no more writings about the Scots by either Pictish or Welsh sources until Aedan comes onto the scene in AD 575.

The 11th battle is at a place called Agned. Once more, historians are unanimous that this too was in Pictland. The location is said to be near Edinburg, and again it is another victory for King Arthur. What is very interesting at this point is both the *Tigernach* of the Irish and the *Pictish Chronicles* suddenly go quiet for the next 40 years. They seem to follow the exact format as the ASC in that if the local army suffers a defeat, there is nothing reported. The two sources seem to support that something of a serious nature did occur in the early sixth century to silence the local scribes. From an archaeological perspective, there are no more expansions by either kingdom until King Aedan comes to the throne. It certainly gives great credence to what Nennius claimed was true.

The Great Battle of Badon

Everything points to the fact that Arthur, like Harold Godwinson after fighting at Agned, had to race back down to Wales. This one time it does make sense. As pointed out earlier, Cerdic had more than enough time to make a pact with Ælle. It is likely the two of them were kept abreast of Arthur's victories, and it looked like it was either now or never. The question is, Which way did the combined armies come? Archaeology seems to be our best source for an answer. Excavation has proven the Anglo-Saxons had made it into Somerset in the middle of the sixth century via the Thames river valley. There is no evidence to support that it was an amphibious assault, as Alan Wilson believes. Therefore unless one day better evidence comes to light, we have to go with an overland assault by the Anglo-Saxon forces. If Bath was indeed the location of the battle, it would appear Arthur got there in the nick of time.

The exact spot of the battle in the Badon region is said to be at Little Solsbury Hill, about two kilometres north-east of Bath. It is a plateau hill that rises 190 metres in a triangular shape with about 500 square metres at the top. It is sloped on all sides at an average angle of 30 degrees. It's definitely defendable, and an army trying to crest it would have a difficult time. The site today is a popular tourist attraction, with absolutely no historical plaques to say this was where Arthur fought the Saxons. There were 4 archaeological and geographical surveys done at the site, the last one by John Oswin in

2012. The results were not one speck of anything from the Dark Ages found here. Therefore, if a battle did take place here, it was cleaned up with uncanny precision.

The story of the battle is exactly dated to AD 515, and it lasted for three days. Arthur is credited by Nennius as have personally killed 960 Saxons in the fight. He also distinguished the Christian religion here with the marking of the cross on his shield. This may be a little propaganda because in those days, each soldier owned his own shield and weapons. It was customary that the family markings would be on them for two reasons. The first one was so people would know if the warrior was heroic, and the second was if he fell in battle, they would know who he was. It is highly unlikely a soldier would give that up for a common religious symbol such as the cross.

Arthur's cavalry was described as being the saviours of the day. They continuously swept around the hill, fending off the Saxons at every location. Thus, the Britons, who were likely the smaller force, saved the day with their quickness. I personally can't see how a horse sitting so high on a hill could be of any use. The rider would have to sweep really low to hit anyone with his sword, not to mention practically falling off his horse to strike down at his opponent. Yet somehow, they pulled it off. I would be more inclined to think the archers would have done the most damage, because the range would have been incredible on a high, sloping hill. However, there is no account of archers being present. The subject of archers has been my conjecture all along based on the different locations at which Nennius says Arthur fought. Horses fighting in thick forest of Scotland without archers would have been suicide for Arthur. Scotland today still has some really dense forest in its southern regions, so if Arthur fought in any one of them without archers, he was certainly at a disadvantage. Thus, based on my knowledge of Dark Ages warfare, I am inclined to believe Nennius, like Geoffrey, did a fair bit of embellishment here.

One thing is for certain: When it was over, the news of the battle swept the whole of the British Isles. Accounts of the battle are repeated by all three great monks—Gildas, Bede and Nennius. Also, the battle is noted by a variety of different annals and chronicles by the Picts, Irish and British. Archaeologists and historians say the research definitely proves the advancements by the Picts, Scots and Saxons came to a halt for at least 20 years at approximately the same time. As Francis Pryor said in his BBC documentary of the Arthurian age, someone stopped them all in their track, and if it wasn't Arthur, then who was it? I think that is the most fitting way of putting it. To date, no historian has come up with an acceptable alternative to this conundrum.

8

The Rocky Road to Camlann

There may be many methods by which truth and justice can be protected. But the only truly efficient way to do it is with cold steel. And God help any kingdom foolish enough to forget it.

—Mordred, *The Legends of Prince Valiant*

Just because you can't find it doesn't mean it didn't happen. Badon is not the only historical site experts can't find.

—unknown British author

The year is AD 937, and King Ragnal of Danelaw is seriously upset. King Olaf Guthfrithson of Dublin has just declared himself High King of all the Vikings in both Ireland and Briton. Suddenly, Ragnal is reduced to a subservient king, and he is not very happy about it. As it is, Ragnal calls for help from King Aethelstan of the Anglo-Saxons Confederation. The 4 separate Anglo-Saxon kingdoms have united into one kingdom of English-speaking people. For Aethelstan, this is a brilliant opportunity to go further and include the Norseman in Northumbria, truly unifying the whole of the island. Therefore with no hesitation, he quickly obliges Ragnal's acquis.

Unfortunately, Aethelstan is unaware that two of his newest acquisitions to the Anglo confederacy are declaring their independence

who basically copied what Nennius wrote, says in his *Ecclesiastical* that the Britons fell into civil war. It would appear modern historians cannot quite agree on who is right.

The reason for the modern-day confusion lies once again in understanding the Celtic culture. In this particular example, the Celtic Ard-Ri institution must be reviewed once more. By now it should be acknowledged that the Britons fully embraced their Celtic identity before and after the Roman period. As mentioned, the Britons took a more Germanic approach to their Dux Bellorum office. Now that the war was over, Arthur could go home, and the petty kingdoms would go back to the way they were before the Saxons had attacked, just like what happened with Arminius of Germany in AD 17, after the Battle of Teutoburg Forest. The German tribes were thankful for him helping them defeat the Romans, but then it was time for everyone to go home. Proposing to rearrange the political infrastructure to anticipate future Roman problems was out of the question. The Celtic mentality simply would not tolerate it. This was the case with Arthur in Briton.

With Badon over, two Welsh kings in particular are determined to have the Ynys Prydein confederacy disbanded and immediately go back to the way things were. These two men were Constantine of Dumonia and Maelgwyn of Gwynedd. It's not openly said whether either of these men were with Arthur in the last 10 or so years, but it certainly is implied. No sooner do these men get home than they decide it time to expand their borders. To Gildas, who was there, it was seen as a typical Celtic cross-border raiding nonsense that has plagued the Celtic culture for centuries. This line of thinking is supported from a famous story out of Ireland called the *Tain Bo Cuailnge* (*The Cattle Raid of Cooley*). This is a story of a cattle raid by the Queen of Connaught (Maeve) to get her hands on a prized bull that was in Ulster. Though by modern perspective it seems like a ludicrous event, back then in the Celtic world, cattle was the most prized possession. Going to war over it was regarded as normal behaviour. Then, 160 years after, Bede the Venerable (who was more an Anglo-Saxon than a Briton) took a completely different view of Gildas's writing and interpreted that it was war. This again is where, when you are not familiar with the culture, you can easily take an extreme view of things. From what I have read, a lot of writers have done just that.

Now, having said all that, the following is likely to prove Bede may have been right.

Apparently, a new subconfederacy is started to fight Constantine and Maelgwyn, clearly implying there was more than what Gildas perceived. The new confederacy was comprised of Glamorgan, Demetae and Powy. King Arthur is again elected to lead this smaller organization. Constantine aggressively took over Dumonia after King Mark passed away. King Mark is famous for the legendary story of Tristan and Isolde. Apparently, Isolde was genuinely King Mark's real wife. Tristan looks like he was a fictional character. There is not much on Mark other than succeeding King Geraint. He didn't last very long; legend has it he was killed by the Irish in one of their raids. Some address him as Constantine III so they don't mix him up with the Roman Constantine who went to Gaul in AD 405. Constantine III was a brutal, lecherous tyrant who was accused of sodomy, adultery and murder of two children. Both Gildas and Bede pour all sorts of venom all over this man. He is recorded in the Welsh Annals as having attacked Erging[4] several times. This is a small kingdom that straddles Dumonia and Glywysing. King Erb (of Erging) went to Arthur for protection against Constantine, and apparently it worked. In the end, Constantine is murdered by Aurelius Caninus, who is not much better, but it does prove the kingdom was in a quandary.

Maelgwyn, whom Gildas called the Dragon of all Tyrants, was perhaps the worst. When he got home from Badon, assuming he was there—and some fictional writers do say he was—he began attacking the neighbouring kingdom of Powy. As a more ruthless character, he had better control of his kingdom and was able to quickly deal with assassins and usurpers in the most horrific means possible. He murdered members of his family and sexually assaulted any woman he pleased. At least, that is the impression you get from Gildas. The one thing we learn about Maelgwyn was, like his grandfather Cunedda (who came down from Gododdin in AD 438 and evicted the Irish out of Ordovices), he was persistent and came to even annoy Arthur himself. Eventually the two men would come to meet in a tragic battle.

---

[4]   The official status of Erging is it is a subkingdom of both Glywysing and Dumonia.

Unlike Mike Ashley, in his book *King Arthur: The Man and the Legend Revealed,* I am deliberately staying away from Geoffrey Monmonth's interpretations of post-Badon Briton. To put it mildly, Geoffrey embellished this part in the Arthur legend with fantastic Technicolor. I'd prefer to keep him out of the equation because things will start to go in all sorts of different directions.

Powy, as we remember, is a long country that stretches the width of Wales through its centre. In terms of land space, it is the largest. In AD 515, it was ruled by a King Aurelius Conanus, or as the Welsh referred to him, King Cynan. There is not much on him either, but Gildas calls him the Lion Beast. He is taking the brunt of Maelgwyn's attacks, and so like the King of Erging has joined in an alliance with Arthur as well. Historically geographers don't show there is much change in border size, so I gather Conanus was able to hold his own.

Up in the north-west corner of Wales, in the region of modern Chester, there emerged a small new kingdom known as Rhos. It was ruled by a king named Cuneglas, or in Welsh Cynlas. Because it was a small kingdom, Gildas referred to him as the Little Dog tyrant.

Down in the south-west corner is the Irish kingdom of Demetae. Officially, Demetae is not part of the Ynys Prydein confederacy; however, there have been numerous examples where the small kingdom joined with the Britons to fight off the Saxons. Though it is not recorded, it is implied they were part of the fight at Badon. At this time, it was ruled by King Vortipor, who was called the Tyrant of Demetae. He is accused of killing his wife and raping his daughter. In the *Demetia Pedigrees* and chronicles, Vortipor lives to the age of 60 and is credited as being in the "Age of Arthur."

Here is something very interesting to note about Gildas in his *De Excidio et Conquestu Britanniae (On the Ruin and Conquest of Britain)*, from which all the tyrants are named. When it comes to condemnation of the Ynys Prydein kings—or as he calls them, the Beasts of Britain—he names all them except the King of Glywysing. You have to go to the royal pedigree of Glywysing to find out who he is. It turns out the man is King Arthur. How did Arthur avoid Gildas's rath? The answer is that Gildas lived in Glywysing, and when you check the Llandaff charter at the Llandaff Cathedral, you find the reason why. In many of the margins are found land grants that were given to the Church of Wales by King Arthur, and so it was obvious Gildas was not going to bite the hand that supported his dioceses.

However, he does sneak in a comment that Mike Ashley and a few others catch, and that is there was one tyrant he considers an overall "bear" to the other British Beasts. The meaning of the name Arthur is bear. Seeing there is no other ruler left in Ynys Prydein to make accusations against other than Arthur, it could only be a reference to him. What's more, this amusing observation is found in Christopher A. Snyder's book *An Age of Tyrants,* and Arthwy (Arthur) is identified are Meurig's son (of Glywysing) but is not listed as a tyrant. This is yet another author's research that says Arthur of Badon is Arthur ap Muerig.

Snyder implies in his book that all the tyrants named had direct dealings with Arthur when he was Dux Bellorum. This was something I needed to know. They say the Welsh kings did accompany Arthur on his campaign, so it is plausible these men were with him. What must to be noted now is that all of these men are accused by Gildas as men without any morals or scruples. It is interesting that they selected Arthur to lead their campaign against the Picts, Scots and Saxons. If we try to be just a little bit honest, does it not make sense that Arthur's traits were pretty much the same as theirs, to have been selected as their military leader? I doubt very much they would have selected a saint like Saint Samson to lead them into battle. Arthur had to have been just as crude and even rougher in nature than they were in order to keep a firm grip on them. Remember that it was a loose confederacy. Any one of them could have pulled out at any time. The fact is that when Badon was over, they quickly did pull out and at once started attacking each other. The Ard-Ri office was immediately terminated. The Welsh annals say Maelgwyn tried to exert himself as Ard-Ri, but officially it was never recognized. Bede gives the full impression Wales, for all intents and purposes, in a state of civil war. Thus Arthur, who is in the mix of all this, is clearly nowhere near the knight in shining armour as Geoffrey of Monmouth portrays him to be. If anything, his closet is probably just as full of despicable atrocities as his counterparts.

The Dark Ages were extremely rough times; murder was probably laughed at, especially when dealing with the Saxons. They were seen as animals and were treated as such. The Picts mostly fought in the nude, and if they won a battle, they would slice off the heads of their enemies and put them up on pikes as trophies. Yes, this is the real world in which Arthur lived. There was no Camelot, royal courts, princesses in embroidered gowns or knights in shining armour. Most men did not even have all their teeth, and they probably stank something awful. If Gildas is even half right about what he wrote, everything was nothing short of horrific. And to think that Arthur was at the top of this kind of society. Francis Pryor, in his research, found that by AD 515 all the Roman civitas were completely abandoned, and with them any semblance of an orderly society. In the new world, you had to be terrifying and crude if you were going to survive. In order for Arthur to survive, he would have had to blend in. This is the kind of man I can see Maelgwyn, Cynas and Constantine respecting, and because he could kill better than all three of them put together, he easily won the position of Dux Bellorium.

Now let's address Camelot. Was it in Caerleon or Cadbury Castle? These two locations are getting the most debate, so it would seem they are the ones to examine. Caerleon is a former Roman garrison in Isca, in south-east Wales, and as far as Geoffrey of Monmouth is concerned, this was undoubtedly the magical kingdom. Cadbury Castle is in Somerset, about 30 kilometres south of Bristol. This is an extremely massive and old Celtic fortress built circa 3000 BC. Archaeologists confirm that once the Romans left Caerleon, it was never reoccupied by the locals. The Silures, who were the dominant Celtic tribe (which became the Glywysing Kingdom), continued to occupy their capital at Dinas Powys, south-west of Cardiff, right up to the end of the 7th century[5]. The Silures, typical of most Britons, went back to their old ways once the Romans left. From this alone, it makes it easy to decide that if there was a Camelot, the place was Cadbury Castle.

Cadbury Castle went through a major excavation by Professor Leslie of Alcock University of Glascow in 1972, and in 1995 he published his findings. To date, no one has been able to revival his work. Therefore we are compelled to go by his findings when it comes to the details on the fortress. Cadbury Castle is a triangular-shaped fortress similar in design as Maiden Castle. It's about 150 metres high, occupying about 7.28 hectares of land. It was originally occupied by the Urnfield people, and then when the Celts came, it was taken over

---

[5]   It's another point to support the Celtic position on the Arthur legend. When the Romans left, all the former Celtic capitals were quickly reoccupied, if they weren't already occupied.

by the Durotriges tribal nation. In the 6th century, the fortress went through a major upgrade when the main gate was made of stone. At this time, an enormous wooden-framed hall was erected that could house several hundred people. Leslie's observations are that it was a major gathering point for the entire establishment. In the centre of the hall was found evidence of a fire pit, thus verifying that when people came to assemble in this place, it was done in a large, circular group. There was no head table, so to speak, as was the case at Tara's grand hall in Ireland. Nor was there a head chair for the king, as was found in the Viking Fortress Hall of Trelleborg, Denmark. The makings of a round table were, in its origins, a circle around a large fire. Arthur reigned over of a small Welsh kingdom like all his counterparts, and so after coming into Cadbury Castle, he had the same status as everyone else. He would have sat in the circle with all the other Welsh kings with no special privileges, and he would have looked just as grubby as they did, sitting on a dirt floor.

The enormous size of Cadbury Castle would have been ideal for assembling the different groups and agreeing to who was to become the Dux Bellorum; as was likely the case when the great 12-battle campaign took place. Thus, again in AD 539 when the kings were frustrated with Maelgwyn, particularly Cynan, the Triads indicate that Maelgwyn had managed by this time to conquer the entire Irish seashore line of Powy and was now posing a threat to Demetae.

Besides the fact Cynan wanted his land back, there was a bigger problem: whether Maelgwyn would raid or attack Demetae, which was upsetting the Irish in general. According to the research done by Rodney Castleden, Vortipor had been well aware of the shoreline advances made by Maelgwyn, and so he advanced his armies so that half of the shore region was now occupied by Demetae. No doubt this posed a serious problem for everyone; the relative peace they had enjoyed for the last 20 years from outside threats could dissipate. Arthur would have quickly understood this and realised Maelgwyn had to be confronted quickly.

I think at this point we must address the subject of Mordred. Up until recently, I thought maybe Mordred had been a mispronunciation or a deliberate name-changing of Maelgwyn by Geoffrey of Monmouth, as he did with Merlyn. In real time, everything that is written at this point points to Maelgwyn as being the villain. However, from Adrian Gilbert's book *The Holy Kingdom,* we find there is a real genealogy for Mordred. He was not made up. Apparently, the claim that Mordred was Arthur's nephew is true. Mordred is related to Arthur on his mother's side (see the family chart below). Once again, from another family relationship subject, Arthur is precisely dated in the 5th and 6th centuries. This Arthur had a son named Morgan. When we look at what the legend says about Arthur and his illegitimate son (Mordred), we know this is made up; likely the source was Chretien de Troyes. Mordred, whom Alan Wilson says was the real villain, is not correct. The real historical records don't show Mordred in anything. He may have accompanied his uncle to the battle of Camlann, but that is about it. I know that for a lot of people who have been conditioned to believing Mordred is who caused all the problems leading up to Camlann, they must be devastated by this news. You may want to review the first chapter, where Chretien was specifically commissioned to create a story of infidelity by Guinevere. He was the one who turned Mordred in the central villain. He got away with the story and making it almost true by taking the Guinevere, who was the real wife of Arthur Mac Aedan and is dated to AD 575.

Now that we have a real sense of the Dark Ages, it's not hard to visualize Cynan, Cynlas, Erb, Arthur and possibly Vortipor sitting around the fire in the great, musty wooden hall at Cadbury and discussing the Cunedda rogue. Taking on Maelgwyn was going to be difficult. His kingdom was up in the Snowdonia Mountains, and there is no doubt if Vortipor was at the meeting, he would have told the others the terrain alone would be difficult to navigate. Also, Arthur is not a young man anymore; his spark for a fight has long since gone. After 20 years of relative peace, Arthur is in the same boat as Ambrosius was: he will have to make a concerted effort to get into this fight.

Now that we have established that Maelgwyn (not Mordred) is what initiated the last great battle, it makes it easy to figure out where the Camlann actually took place. Norma Goodrich's research of Camlann being along Hadrian's Wall is now clearly out of the question. She doesn't stand alone on this point, because there are others who say the same thing, but she is the most prominent on the issue. The problem with Hadrian's Wall as the location, which is identified as Camboglan, is it's deep in Scotti territory. It doesn't make any sense that if Mordred was the villain, Arthur would be allies with the Scots. Slaughter Bridge in Cornwall, as Geoffrey of Monmouth claimed, is outright dismissed. Archaeologists have already checked out the spot, and nothing was found. As it is, wherever Camlann is, it has to be somewhere in Wales and likely some in the north-west of Wales.

It turns out there are two places in Wales very close to each other and ideally located on the Gwynedd Powy border; both are called Camlan. The first one has three locations crowded together: Camlan Isaf, Bron Camlan and Camlan Uchof. It is on the Dyfi River on the very southern edge of the Snowdonia National Park, about 25 kilometres east of the coastal town of Barthmouth. The locals were so confident this is the famous Camlann battle site that they even place a monument stone to mark the area. Authors like Rodney Castleden and Chris Barber have mentioned the spot as being a very plausible location for where the battle took place. The second location is about seven kilometres south-east of Barmouth, just past the Penny Cader Mountain. Adrian Gilbert and Alan Wilson support this location.

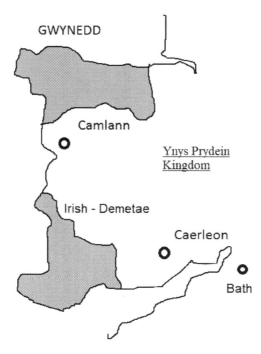

"Map of Dark Age Wales"

9

The Battle and Arthur's Disappearance

A ship with shields before the sun,
Six maidens round the mast,
A red-gold crown on every one,
A green gown on the last.

The fluttering green banners there
Are wrought with ladies' heads most fair,
And a portraiture of Guenevere
The middle of each sail doth bear.

A ship with sails before the wind,
And round the helm six knights,
Their heaumes are on, whereby, half blind,
They pass by many sights.

The tatter'd scarlet banners there
Right soon will leave the spear-heads bare.
Those six knights sorrowfully bear
In all their heaumes some yellow hair.

—William Morris, "Near Avalon"

According to Legend, after the battle of Camlann, Arthur
was taken away by 9 Faery Queens to the island of Avalon
(Island of Apple) and recovered from his wounds.

Apparently, the date of the battle is accurately dated to AD 537 from the *Annals of Cambria*. The way the battle is described, it was an ambush. Using Taliesin's poem on the battle, not only was it an ambush in a thick forest, but it happened near a bridge. Sounds to me it has all the makings of another Stirling Bridge slaughter, as was conducted by William Wallace. It is more than likely Arthur came into Gwynedd with an army much larger than Maelgwyn's. It's likely Maelgwyn did accompany Arthur on his 12-battle campaign, and as such he picked up on many of Arthur's strategies. Therefore, Maelgwyn's only hope was to use the terrain to his advantage. If we suppose that he played the same kind of card as what happen at Stirling, then half of Arthur's army was allowed to cross the bridge before Maelgwyn attacked from both sides of the road. One thing must be remembered: when it comes to travelling in Briton, the Roman roads were still in good shape.

As it is, we don't know how the battle took place. Neither do we know whether Arthur was wounded or killed in the battle. J. E. Lloyd, in *The Death of Arthur,* is very insistent on this point. However, with the events that follow after the battle, it does stand to reason Arthur was injured, to say the very least, and he likely did not survive them.

In such thick forests, as is described by Taliesin, it's not very hard to smuggle Arthur away from the battle. Smuggling Arthur out of the battle without anyone knowing does have a believable argument to it. From what we learn of Maelgwyn in his attempt to usurp the High King position after the battle, that clearly tells us he was not clued in on the situation. Everyone else was aware that if word got out Arthur was dead, the Saxons would take advantage of it. From both legend and in reality, the battle of Camlann ended in a disaster, and the Unys Prydein confederacy was extremely vulnerable. The other kingdoms, including Dumonii, quickly unified like never before to prevent Maelgwyn from taking over, and to make every effort that all outsiders, especially the Saxons, would discover Arthur was critically wounded or even dead. It may be from this collusion that the legend he was only sleeping and will one day awake took shape.

Now comes the biggest mystery of the Arthur legend: What became of him? Two of the main sources I used here were Rodney Castleden and Adrian Gilbert, who was assisted by Alan Wilson and Baram Blackett. One thing is for sure: despite all the speculations that take place, no archaeological excavation has yet to take place to prove any of the following theories. Now that this is understood, we can begin.

The first theory of where Arthur was taken is Bardsey Island. Bardsey Island was a monastic island about 30 kilometres west of Bartmouth. If Arthur came here and was seriously wounded, chances are the monks would have made some kind of effort to bandage him up or at least do something to ease his pain.

The next spot that is claimed is the Island of Whithorn. It's not really an island but more of a peninsula up in the western region of Gododdin. Here, there is a considerable amount of debate that Arthur not only came here but stayed the winter before he travelled back to his own kingdom in Glamorgan. Those who are following this story will definitely draw the conclusion Arthur survived the battle but was not in very good shape for travelling.

The final location where it is believed Arthur may have gone is the Isle of Man. Here many a historian has played with the word Avalon, Island of Apples. The native Gaelic spoken on the island is called Manx. It is said to be a form of Brythonic Gaelic. Some experts feel that Geoffrey's Avalon was likely on the Isle of Man because there is a section of the island that is covered in apple orchards. But once again, no one has done serious research to know whether there is any legitimacy to this claim.

Now that the word Avalon has been mentioned, we are compelled to address the Glastonbury Cathedral myth—because that is exactly what it is, and nothing more. It is beyond certain that King Arthur was never at the famed cathedral. Yet I know, as does most of the world, it is the greatest tourist location when looking for King Arthur's burial. They still have a plaque marking where he was found. The true story about Arthur and Glastonbury is that circa AD 1188, the great cathedral suffered a terrible fire that damaged most of the building. The monks were desperate to find the cash to restore their beautiful church. As it was, Henry II gave them their golden opportunity of salvage. Someone told King Henry of the folklore concerning Arthur's curse of coming back to life. It made a deep impression on him, and Henry ordered that the body of Arthur be found at once. When the word reached the ears of the Glastonbury monks, they swiftly went to work to fabricate an event to capture the imagination of the king. They cut out an oak tree trunk and placed the skeletons of a male and female body in it. Then they designed a small pewter cross with the inscription, "*Here lies the renowned King Arthur.*" It is too bad Henry did not know too much about things that have aged; if he did, he would have quickly realised the wooden box should have been rotten to the point of unrecognition. However, he was fooled into believing the hoax created by the monks was true, and he gave the monastery a handsome reward for their work. To this very day, there are still hundreds if not thousands of King Henrys being duped by the monastery.

Now for the last and maybe the most plausible conclusion to what became of Arthur. According to local tradition in modern Glamorgan, when Arthur did die, they wanted to continue the mystery of no one knowing anything of his disappearance. As it was, the last journey of King Arthur fell into the hands of Saint Iltud, a cousin of Arthur. Geoffrey of Monmouth claims Saint Iltud is the one who conducted Arthur's coronation ceremony. There may be some merit to that considering this part of Wales was said to be the most Christianized part of Briton in the Dark Ages. The story goes that Saint Iltud buried Arthur up in the mountains of Mynydd Caer, just west of Cardiff. Up in this mountain range is the remains of a small church, where an amateur excavation was conducted. They claimed to have been found a mixed metal brass cross with Arthur's name on it. The church's name is Saint Peter's. Those involved with the excavation tried to get archaeological authorities to verify the discovery, but to date they have been unsuccessful.

Whether any of the above is true, one thing is certain: keeping Arthur's death a secret did work to the Ynys Prydein's advantage. The Picts, the Scots and the Saxons did not advance out of their borders until AD 550. The Saxons carried on in their drive west but made very slow progress. The Anglos were a lot more successful, driving north on account of the Scots attacking the Picts. By AD 600 what is now known as England was fully taken. However, the three groups once more did not get any farther. For a brief while, Aethfrith managed to take Gododdin, but that only lasted for his life, and it was taken when again it was under the Gododdin kingship.

10

Arthur's Genealogy: King Tewdrig, King Meurig and the Family Saints

The Sky is blue because
the dancing fairies
paint it blue from dawn to dust,
at night,
The reason why the sky is grey,
is because
the night goblins kill the bright blue light.
So why is the sky blue?
Maybe because of me and you.

—Haley

W hen Merlyn entered the gates of Tintagel, Uther and Ygraine were excited to see him. They had for him wonderful news of their newborn child, Arthur. However, it was because of that news that Merlyn had come to the castle. He wasn't going to mince his words on the issue, and so he came out and said it: he was here to take the child away. Ygraine was devastated and confused, and she clung desperately to her newborn baby. "Why does Merlyn want to take him away?" Merlyn had only to look at Uther Pendragon, and the king knew at once he had made a pact with Merlyn for being allowed to seduce the Duke of Cornwall's wife. Slowly but forcibly, he pulled the young Arthur from the screaming arms of Ygraine and gave the child to Merlyn.

That is the story that the whole world knows regarding the origins of King Arthur. If there is any other story about his beginnings, it is not known, except for those who hang around Alan Wilson. As many in Wales know, for the last 40 or more years, Alan Wilson has been telling quite a different story on the true King Arthur, and to date it has still not been recognized. I stumbled upon the man only when I came across my first big date discrepancy on the Arthur of the late 5th century. Once conventional academics took a firm position on a variety of different aspects of the Arthur of Badon, my curiosity was at once piqued. My background is in mechanical engineering, and for me, the numbers have to add up right. I found that in the world of history, such exactness is not always the case. Many historians, especially when it comes to King Arthur, deliberately avoid putting down dates to verify their versions of story, not realizing what they just said doesn't make any sense because someone like me always tries to keep things in mathematical order.

Two dates are firm in the minds of most British historians when it comes to King Arthur. The first one is AD 515, the date accepted by all as when the Battle of Badon took place. A large majority of historians agree Arthur likely had fought at this battle against the Saxon warlord Cerdic. The second is AD 537, the date on which the Battle of Camlann took place. Officially they don't know who fought at it, but the only name they got to work is King Arthur. After some 1,500 years, the greatest minds of Great Britain have still not been able to come up with an alternative, so they are stuck with Arthur.

King Tewdrig

Now the fun begins. From everything I have read, there are more than a dozen authors who claim the Arthur of Badon from a historical perspective is the son of a King Meurig. They are pretty firm on this point. King Meurig was the king of Glywysing, which later becomes Gwent under Arthur's rule. He is the son of King Tewdrig. As I have mentioned before, as long as no one mentions any dates, this little sequence of genealogy is quickly accepted by all with no problem! You can go the Llandaff Cathedral in the North Choir and see for yourself the beautiful stained-glass windows of the three great kings lined up in a row—grandfather, father and son. Everybody in south-east Wales accepts this point as common knowledge, just as you and I accept the fact that the moon circles the earth.

Now for the baffling part that comes when opening a conventional history book. Because Arthur of Badon is without reservation born in AD 478, then it is a simple math case, as Chris Gidlow puts it. Apply the generation rule to the father and grandfather to approximate their dates of birth. A generation is measured at 25–30 years. This would mean King Meudrig was born circa AD 453. King Tewdrig was born circa AD 427. This is common sense. So like I said, I looked at my first historical reference via the Internet, and I find King Tewdrig, father of Meurig, was born in AD 600. His son is born in AD 575. As soon as I see this, I am completely baffled. Did no one see this glaring typo when they posted it? I checked another reference on King Tewdrig, and in this one he is dated in AD 476, but there is no mention of his sons, his marriage or anything. How convenient. I check another source, and it is said King Tewdrig is a saint and is dated to AD 625. As I go through dozens of different sources, one thing becomes painfully clear: King Tewdrig's date of birth is not accurately written down by any of the official sources. Research done by Terry Beaverton, in *Wales, Historical Companion,* has the most realistic date of birth, circa AD 406.

The next stage is to see what is written about the man. The first source claims Tewdrig was around at the time the Romans first pulled out of Briton. Everybody in Great Britain knows the date of that as AD 410, so that one isn't hard to guess. However, the reference has no specifics as to whether Tewdrig was a boy or a man—only that he was alive when the legions were pulling out. Another story that is more famously known is of the Saxon attack on Glywysing by the sea. Again, in this story there are no dates. The author, who I am sure does not want to be named, says the attack happened at the time when King Geraint was the king of Dumnonia. King Geraint was not the king of Dumonia until after Ambrosius was dead in AD 475. That does not make any sense, and clearly the author is taking some rather extreme liberties of his reader's ignorance. Finally, there is a story of when King Tewdrig wants to abdicate the thrown to his son Meudrig, but Meudrig is not interested in the offer. There is no date when this event took place either, but what does verify with this source is the author is insistent that Meurig is definitely Tewdrig's son. Thus the stained-glass windows and these two men are confirmed as related. The story of the three men is consistent, but not their dates.

You can go on the Internet and see there are dozens of pictures of what King Tewdrig looked like. The most notable ones show him dressed in chainmail with a simple band around the head for a crown. Someone did a wood carving of the man at Tindern Old Station of Monmouthshire. Here, we can get probably the best likeness of what the man really was: long beard, rough looking and simple but warm clothing in a time where there was very little in the way of comfort. If I were to take a guess at this sculpture, it is definitely 5th century. Thus, the image of him is also consistent with the alleged time frame.

Tewdrig's full name is Tewdrig ap Tailfailt. He was the king of Glywysing. All historians are in agreement on this. That also helps the time frame for Glywysing because it had only a brief historical period when it was broken into Glamorgan and Gwent. His identity is said to be fully recorded in the *Llandaff Book*. He was a warrior-king of Silurian background, and so he likely vicious when in battle. He is credited as being Christian and defending the faith throughout his life. It does give credit to Nennius, saying his grandson Arthur was Christian, and so we now know from where Arthur inherited his religious beliefs. He was born in Garth Madryn, Brechonshire, Wales. Breconshire is just north of Glywysing in the Powy Kingdom, later to become Gwent. Tewdrig was married to Prawst verch Gwrgan of Erging. Erging, you will recall, is a small kingdom that straddles the Severn River. On one side is Glywysing, and on the other is Dumnoni. In personality, Tewdrig is described as a wise and sensible man who was very loyal to his family. There are no arguments that Meudrig, his son, had great admiration and respect for his father. Clearly, he was a very different character to the reckless King Cunneda of Gwynedd, who was the great-grandfather of Maelgwyn. There is no date for the Battle of Titern on the Wye River, but it is where Tewdrig met his end, fighting off a Saxon naval assault. Meurig ap Tewdrig succeeds him as king of Glywysing. St. Tewdrig Church on the Wye River is the resting place of King Tewdrig. His grave was verified in 1614 by a Francis Godwin. Thus, it is without question that King Tewdrig is a real historical figure.

King Meurig

There is a lot written on King Meurig ap Tewdrig, and from it comes another realistic date of his birth as circa AD 460, again from Terry Beaverton's research. I can't help but notice that on a major website like The Celtic Kingdoms of the British Isles, they have Meurig's date of birth in AD 625. How can you be that far off when Tewdrig is registered in the early 5th century? This is the kind of nonsense I have been going through to verify whether there really were any King Arthurs in the late 5th century. The most written on Meurig is found in the *Llandaff Charter*. Meurig had done a lot for the Church in his time, and of course all his actions were well-recorded. From them alone we can have yet another source of reference for dates.

In the *Llandaff Charter*, the earliest records show Muerig as being very generous in land grants to Church officials like Cyngen, abbot of Carvan, and Cadgen, abbot of St Iltud. The most serious entry is when Muerig was excommunicated by Bishop Oudoceus for killing the priest Cynfeddw. Meurig endured the excommunication for about two years when he asked for a pardon. It was granted, and as penance King Muerig gave another land grant to the Church. Another entry shows Muerig making a concerted effort to financially support Saint Dubricius in the restorations of Llandaff Cathedral. All of the Church persons mentioned here are real, historical people. From them we again have yet more verification of the time frame, particularly with Saint Dubricius. He is dated from AD 465 to 550. His dates give credibility to the research done by Terry Beaverton. Also, the mentioning of *Dubricius* by Geoffrey of Monmouth properly dates his story of Arthur as well.

You get the impression the Church in south-east Wales is very well-established and has a high degree of authority in the royal courts. Such ecclesiastical authority does not happen in the Saxon kingdoms until Henry II circa AD 1133 (the Becket Incident). It shows how the advanced Christianity movement in Wales progressed.

King Meurig was married to an Onbrawst ap Gwrgan and had 8 children: Arthwy (Arthur), Madoc, Frioc, Idnerth, Pawl, Gwenowy, Afrella and Anna. Anna is the most interesting member of the family in verifying King Arthur's dates because she gives birth to two boys, and they both become saints in the Welsh Church: Saint Tathan and

Saint Samson. Saint Samson in particular becomes a Welsh icon up there with Saint David, and so there is a tremendous amount of material on him. King Muerig, like his father Tewdrig, is very endearing to his family, and he pays close attention to all of them to make sure they have lives that enhance the Glywysing Kingdom.

Staying with the family theme just a little bit longer, we learn that much of Tewdrig's sound thinking was passed down to Muerig, especially when it came marrying off his daughters. All of them were very well-planned. Anna was married to King Grawey of Amorica; Amorica is another word for the country Brittany in Gaul. This is an enormous political piece of success on Muerig's part. His second daughter, Gwenowy, was married to King Hen of Erging. In this move, Muerig physically has the two kingdoms of Glywysing and Erging united. His third daughter, Afrella, was married to Prince Umbrafel of Emyr Llyrdow, a subkingdom of Amorica. Through marriages alone, Muerig vastly improved the political influence of his kingdom.

We find again from the *Llandaff Charter* that Muerig's most favourite son was indeed Arthwy. As stated before, land grants were a serious issue of all kings at this time, and they weren't given out lightly. When you see that the churches kept strict records of the land grants they received, you know how serious it was. The records show that when Arthwy came of age, his father trusted him with the subject, and on several occasions, there are records that the Church received land grants by Arthwy on behalf of his father, Muerig. From this it was obvious Muerig was grooming his eldest son to succeed him as king. This was further evidence that Arthwy was Meurig's son.

Two things must be noted at this point. The first one is to realise that the Celtic institution of nominating kings has been terminated. This is largely due to the fact the Christian Church had squeezed the Druids out of the political process. It was to the Church's benefit, and to the kings, to promote the royal succession system that was the norm on the main continent. The second point is that a national identity change takes place near the end of Muerig's reign, and Glywysing has its name changed to Gwent. Once Arthur comes to the throne, part of Gwent becomes what we now recognize as Glamorgan. In the *Brut of England,* the second name change is recorded in 1272.

According to John Edward Lloyd in *A History of Wales from the Earliest Times,* Muerig passed away in AD 517. Using Terry Beaverton's research, that would make Muerig 57 years old when he died. When you consider the average age was 40 years old in those days, this is very reasonable. The common understanding in modern Glamorgan is that King Muerig ap Tewdrig is buried at Llandaff Cathedral.

Thus, from the routine official documents alone, we confirmed Arthwy (Arthur) was the son of Muerig and the grandson of Tewdrig. From this, it can be surmised with a great deal of accuracy that Arthur was born in the late fifth century, and that easily makes him the most likely candidate to have been the Arthur of Badon. Only one more step is needed to be absolutely sure we have the right man, and that comes from his nephews and cousins.

The Family Saints

In King Arthur ap Muerig's family tree, there are three canonized saints. I figure these are the anchor to knowing for sure that this Arthur is the Arthur of Badon. The one big thing scholars have been debating the most are the dates when Badon actually took place and whether he could have possibly been there. As mentioned before, we could stop where we are because the evidence so far is more than enough to say the Arthur of Glamorgan fits the bill. However, just to make things interesting, we are going to take it one step further by looking into his own family lineage. In Arthur's family tree, there were three saints: Iltud, Tathan and Samson. We are now going through official Church documents of the Vatican that are recognized as not only genuine but holy. When a person is canonized to the status of saint, it is a very serious event that the Church does not take lightly. The person in question is held up to serious scrutiny, and not only are the dates verified, but the person himself must meet the strict regulations of the honour. Some modern historians may still feel these records can be challenged as well but know that is a serious risk, especially if they make any mistakes. From what I witnessed on the Internet reference, when it came to saints, the dates are exact, and you can instantly see that religious personnel are not punted around as political figures are.

Saint Iltud

Saint Iltud is the son of Bicany (Bicanus) and his wife, Gwerylla ap Tewdrig. He is dated to the middle of the fifth century. Gweylla is the daughter of King Tewdrig. This would make Iltud a first cousin of Arthwy (Arthur). He was a disciple of Germanus of Auxerre, and so it is very likely he was familiar with Saint Patrick. This in itself verifies the time frame, because Saint Patrick is generally accepted to have lived from AD 420 to 460. Before becoming a monk, Iltud was a soldier in the Glywysing army. There are no dates for this time period. Iltud got involved with the Church because he and a few of his men had a run-in with Saint Cadoc. Iltud had a spiritual experience with Cadoc and thus retired from the military to devote his life to the monastic order. He is credited with opening up a number of monasteries in southern Wales, and he schooled such high-profile people as Gildas and Saint Samson. Late in life, he retreated into the mountains of Ewenny, about 11 kilometres west of Cardiff, and for a number of years, he lived in seclusion in a cave. His most noted historical act was that he is credited with the burial of King Arthur. Because there is only one Saint Iltud in Wales, historians do not question this common belief.

Saint Tathan (Athan)

Fully recorded as the son of King Grawey and Anna ap Muerig, Tathan is dated to a period of AD 495. They do not say whether this is his birth date or the time frame in which he lived. I think it may be his birth date considering Arthur is recorded to have been born circa AD 478. This calls into question whether Anna was his older sister, because the dates are very close to each other. Anna is Arthur's sister, and that would make Tathan his nephew. Tathan was born in Gwent, and so though the father is from Amorica. Events unfolded that Anna was able to give birth to her son in her native homeland. He went to Ireland and was trained to be a monk. After that, he returned to Wales and set up a monastic order in Caerwent. His accomplishment in life is his constant devotion to his faith and to education. He died in AD 540 and is buried in Llandwit Major.

Saint Samson

Saint Samson, like Saint Tathan, is the son of Amon and Anna ap Meurig. I assume this might be an earlier marriage before King Grawey. Samson's birth is dated to AD 485, and he was also born in Gwent. He too would be another nephew of Arthur ap Muerig. Something was going on in the family politics, because for a short while he was put under the care of his cousin Saint Iltud. Considering Anna is now married to Grawey, that may have had something to do with it. As we know, her father was an ambitious man, and she no doubt had to play her part in his political goals. Anyway, Samson is raised and educated to become a monk, and a very notable one at that. He was outspoken and very vigilant in promoting the Christian Church. He was ordained a bishop by Bishop Dubricius on February 22, 521. He did a lot of travelling to places like Guernsey, Amorica and Sicily. Circa AD 550, he was part of a major ecclesiastical event in Paris and signed a document that had major importance to his status with the Church. He died in AD 573 and is buried at the Cathedral of Dol in Amorica.

What these three saints do for King Arthur is peg his timeline to the late 5th century. With this, I can now see how many historians have come up with Arthur's birth date as around AD 478. Just for a little humour, we do not know officially when Anna was born. Many of the reference sources I have checked have her birth in AD 535, which is easily seen as incorrect. If the Vatican has someone like Saint Samson's birth carved in stone as AD 485, then the Internet reference sources can easily be dismissed.

What was great about this exercise was verifying from sources the other people who lived around King Arthur, because if it was plausible, then Arthwy ap Muerig is in fact the Arthur of Badon. It turns out he is more than genuine. When I get to my conclusion, I will put it all together, but I think that even at this stage, it's obvious the mystery around the real Arthur is already solved.

11

The Legacy and the Mystery

It was not Sir Lancelot I came for
It was Galahad I should have taken
It was not Guinevere I should have watched
It was Mordred who was the villain
It was Arthur absence that caused the rift
It was Morgause who stole the crown
It was Percival who I did not see
It was the Fisher King who saved our soil
It was Excalibur that disappeared into the watery mist
It was Arthur who became the legendary myth

—"Merlin's Mist," 12th century

If you were standing on the windy shorelines of Dalriada in early spring AD 498, looking west to Antrim of Ireland, you would have noticed a huge fleet of small Viking-designed ships coming toward you. According to the *Tigernach,* Ireland had a national fleet of over 200 ships, and each ship had a minimum crew of 27 sailors, just like their Pictish counterparts. Therefore, at minimum the Irish arrived in Dalriada with an army of about 5,400 men; some historians have raised that number to as high as 10,000. This army was being led by a big, rough-looking, redheaded man named Fergus Mor mac Eirc. He was coming over to formally create a kingdom, and the capital would be Dunadd. Up until this time, Dalriada was only a territory of Antrim Ireland, a Tuathe kingdom of Ulster. King Eirc of Tara had noticed that this territory in Pictland was loosely governed for a considerable amount of time, and it was long overdue for an overhaul. The Picts preferred it this way because they never wanted the Scots to have a permanent base in their lands. With the arrival of Fergus Mor, tension between the Picts and Scots immediately sparked. A major battle took place just outside Dunbarton, and the Picts were soundly beaten. This aggravated the Picts, and so began what British historians refer to as the great Northern Civil War.

I'm not sure how the British historians came up with the term *civil war,* because it was any but. Up until AD 550, it was for the most part a minor feud between the two Gaelic nations, mostly border skirmishes. After that date, other players started getting involved, notably the Angle king Aethelfrith of Bernicia in AD 593. You will recall he took a chance by invading Gododdin and was quickly challenged by Aedan mac Gabrain. Unfortunately, Aedan did not fare well, and suddenly the Angles were now major game players in the region. Aethelfrith does not rule well either in his time, and he makes a serious mistake in attacking his fellow Angles in Deira and the Welsh in Powy circa AD 616. In the Welsh conflict, he ends up being killed in battle. Plus, his sons squander Arthelfrith's successes and lose everything. However, it does not stop the Angles from trying again.

The three-way fighting goes on for the next 300 years, with no one ever getting an upper hand. Things are so unstable that the clerics have very little time to fully record the events as they unfold. As it is, a huge historical void blankets a massive period of time.

Then, just as things couldn't get any worse, in AD 795 the Vikings appear at Lindisfarne. As many will know, the Viking scourge adds another 200 years to the dismal era.

The realization of this incredible void comes when you visit your local library. If you were to ask for a book on the Northern Civil War, chances are the librarian will not know what you are talking about. You will be compelled to give some details on the topic so that the librarian has some idea where to look. As I have found out, on this subject there are no more than 2 or 3 books written. That verifies this enormous conflict had massive repercussions.

The Viking era is a little bit better, but not by much. Only because some people have Romanized them with a few movies, the selection of books are a little more generous. Still, it is kind of embarrassing when you think about it. There are dozens of Viking greats like Rollo, Eric the Red, Harold Blue-Tooth and Cunit, but for the Celts, there are only two great names that stand out: Brian Boru of Ireland and Alfred the Great of Wessex. Both men not only stopped the tide of conquest but also were able to permanently subdue their opponents—something Kink Arthur never accomplished. You might say as far as history was concerned, despite all their pillaging, the Vikings still were the good guys.

The remarkable event occurs when you ask your library for a book on King Arthur, and suddenly you are overwhelmed with selection. There are hundreds of books to choose from when it comes to this man, both historically and fictionally: *The Mist of Avalon* by Marion Zimmer Bradley, *The Winter King* by Bernard Cornwell, *The Taliesen* by Stephen R. Lawhead, *The Skystone* by Jack Whyte, *The Queen of Camelot* by Nancy McKenzie and *The Lady of Shalott* by Alfred Tennyson, just to mention modern writers. Of course, historical writers' manuscripts like Thomas Malory and Chretien de Troyes are still in print. There is an endless supply of historical books as well by Norma Goodwich, Jean Markle, Alan Wilson, Christopher Gidlow and Chris Barber. How is it possible that Alfred the Great and a 500-year-old war can't compete with King Arthur of Camelot?

This is the staggering mystery that evolved out of the legacy.

I believe it started with Geoffrey of Monmouth. When he wrote his *History of the Kings of Britain,* there were half a dozen or so critics who outright said the King Arthur part wasn't true. This unleashed a great search that is still going on to this day. What compounded the mystery was the fundamental problem that the Anglo-Saxon critics lack the understanding of the Celtic culture. Further, they didn't think it was a pertinent subject relevant to solving the Arthur phenomenon. Jean Markle has written volumes on this one point alone. From the Celtic bard perspective, there was an enormous amount of material available prior to Geoffrey of Monmouth; it simply went unnoticed because it was all seen as fictional writing. The relevancy of a bard story was never comprehended. Probably the best example of this kind of writing was the *Twrch Trwyth,* the wild boar story. It was a representational story of a true event. Up until the ninth century, when it was formally written down, it was a Celtic oral tradition story. It was said in such a way that it could be remembered precisely. Lady Charlotte Guest, in her compilation of *Mabinogion,* was the authority in recognizing what was a true bardic story and as such estimating its date of origin. From her alone, they have been able to date hundreds of bardic stories on King Arthur to the 5th century. The best example on this point is the Celtic bard story of the *Tan Bo Cualinge* of Ireland. It has been accurately dated to AD 5–10. When you are not familiar with the trademark style of writing, it is natural to be sceptical of how people can distinguish it. It is like recognizing a Shakespearean play by today's standards. "To be or not to be?" Nearly everyone around the world recognizes this famous quote from the play *Hamlet*. As such, it is common knowledge that the play was written in the 16th century. No one in the English-speaking world would argue this point. The same principle applies with bardic poems. Two of the most powerful examples of this point are the poems of *King Geraint* and Aneirin's *Y Gododdin*. *King Geraint* is dated to the 5th century, and *Y Gododdin* is dated to the 7th century by Celtic experts.

Here's a quick understanding for the bardic story. Take for example the story of Excalibur. The dreamy, supernatural quality to the story is its overall identity. Next is the fact that everything has a magical power to it, like Arthur's sword. When Arthur engages in a dual with Sir Lancelot, he ends up breaking his sword. He approaches Merlin for a replacement because he wants a sword equal to the one he pulled from the stone. Merlin takes him down a small lake and introduces him to the Lady of the Lake. She provides Arthur with another magical sword, this one named Excalibur. This is one of the most memorable, legendary stories of King Arthur, and the way the story is written, it is easy to remember. Where the identity, the reality, and the time of the story comes from is in the background. Francis Pryor has done considerable research into this in order to know how it all works. The concept of water being magical is distinctly a Celtic tradition. A magical representative such as a wizard is also traditionally found in the Druid cult. Lastly, a weapon connected to water is a very common trait of the Celtic world. The tradition is that weapons were thrown into the water rather than being retrieved. This does happen with Arthur and Bedivere, who throws the sword back into the lake after the Battle of Camlann.

The Celtic world for Briton formally ends when Anglo King Aethelstan comes to the throne circa AD 927. Aethelstan is credited with having been the first English king in fully uniting the country under one culture. Other events prior to him assisted him so that when he politically unified the country, all the other events fell into play under the English banner. If King Arthur actually existed, it was before AD 927. Using conventional historical events is another way to narrow the time Arthur existed. For example, the Synod of Whitby of AD 664 represented the specific end of the Celtic Druids. Thus, the time restriction is between the end of the Roman Britannia in AD 410 to Whitby in AD 664. We know that during Roman times, the Celtic culture was suppressed, and previous to the Roman period, there is no mention of Arthur in any Celtic tradition. When you have studied the Celtic culture to the extent Jean Markle has, you can refine this event even more precisely, strictly from a general historical perspective. This needs to be known because when specifying the literature time frame; they are all concentrated in the same period. It turns out the period is completely focused on the early 6th century. The verification is coming from conventional event time restraints. Thus whoever Arthur was, history confines him to the 6th century.

Addressing the literature is Christopher Gidlow, and Norma Goodrich provides one of the most interesting arguments to Arthur's authenticity. The name Arthur starts to appear by as early as AD 575 with Arthur Mc Aedan, and then the name is basically nonstop in just about every *Annals Chronicles*, pedigree and legendary story throughout Briton. By the time Nennius sits down to write his version of British history, there is a wealth of information on Arthur. From the dates of the literature, he has no difficulty in narrowing it down to Arthur to the end of the 5th century and early 6th century. Christopher uses an interesting argument: If Arthur was not the person who fought at Badon and Camlann, then who was? After some 1,500 years, the academic community has still not found a suitable replacement.

What happens after Geoffrey of Monmouth, Jean Markle and Norma Goodrich argue, is an excessive refinement of the original story. From the 12th century to modern times, it is estimated by the University of Wales that there have been more than 30,000 different versions of the Arthurian story. Wikipedia currently has a list of more than 600 books on King Arthur. This is what is officially known. Who knows what the numbers are unofficially? It is undoubtedly the greatest legacy of any person in the history of Great Britain.

Everything points to the fact that Arthur was real, and the evidence points to the fact the man was from the late 5th century. As long as we keep him in wolfskins and chain mail, he's no big deal. However, once we place him in shiny armour and have him chasing after the Holy Grail, like Geoffrey of Monmouth did, the debate of his existence is beyond comprehension. His mystery comes from the fact that people are pursuing a man created from some of the most amazing embellishments in the history of literature. As one Russian scholar put it, when looking at a shiny pearl, always remember at its centre is a grain of dirty sand.

Conclusion of the Quest

Love me or hate me, both are in
my favour ... If you love me, I'll
always be in your heart ... If you
hate me, I'll always be in your
mind.

—William Shakespeare

aking a mountain out of a molehill is not something that
is exclusive to the Celts, but it does appear they were the
best at it. As you saw, Geoffrey of Monmouth was the man
who started the ball rolling, and as Hollywood continues to put out
movies with more versions on the legendary Arthur, yet another layer
of what to believe is created. As I said in my introduction, as far as
books are concerned, the different versions of Arthur's story is simply
off the measuring stick. The University of Wales alone claims to have
more than 40,000 books on King Arthur in its library. One person
would not live long enough to read them all. Because more than 95
percent of them are academic studies on the legend, somebody from
my perspective can overlook them all. The legend only has historical
importance if you want to know how Arthur became so great, and it's
pretty obvious now that Monmouth and de Troye were the reason,
not Arthur.

There was a reason why historians called it the Dark Ages. It
all started with Rome itself being sacked by the Visigoths. Burning
down the libraries and ripping down the great sculptures meant
nothing to them, and once they had their gold, they put the city to the
match and left. Across the entire empire, it was pretty much the same
story everywhere. Franks were pillaging Gaul, Huns were ransacking

Greece and the Irish were invading Wales. Everything was in chaos, and the refined light of advanced culture was being extinguished. It was now the gruesome truth of survival in its rawest form. Where once stood a single emperor, there was now an assorted world of barbarian warlords. Like the gangsters of Detroit in the 1920s, the name of the game was who can get the most territory through the most effective killing. This was the kind of world in which the true King Arthur lived. Bede and Gildus alone give us enough detail in their ranting to prove this point beyond any doubt. The one thing that is amusing about them is they are not going to give any credit to any of the gangsters of their time, regardless of how successful they are, like Arthur at Badon. In a way, we still do the same thing today. If Al Capone did in fact do anything of service for his country, there are very few who know of it. Off the record, Gildus, who did live in Arthur's time, is claimed to have written a book on the Camelot king, but after he completed it, he threw it in the sea. Everything stops there.

Thus, now we know of the period that anyone living in the Dark Ages had to have particular skills to get along with their gangster neighbours like Maelgwn from Gwynned, a man who would rather slit your throat than look at you. Tewtrig showed the trick was in cunning and tenacity—no doubt a trait he successfully passed on to his son, and unfortunately not to Merlin. Thus one of the primary principles of believability is firmly established. Arthur had his father's wit, and seeing how Glamorgan continued to grow, it was clear he was likely the Al Capone of his time. His chief opponents were not his fellow Britons, but the Saxons and the Angles led by Cerdic and Aelle, respectively. These two men were even more ruthless than Maelgwn, if you can believe that. The *Saxon Chronicles* tell how both men fought without stop for 10 years. They had lost as many battles as they won. They kept it up because they figured the trick with the Britons was they always vacated their lands every time it was attacked. Thus all the Saxons had to do was keep up the pressure, and soon all of Briton would fall. Angles and Saxons were grubby smelly and never changed their clothes, so just from their appearance, it was obvious their tactics were the same: smash and grab.

On the other side of the island, you had people no less as despicable as the Saxons but a lot more refined, culturally speaking. They at least knew the importance of washing and eating with a knife instead of one's hands. As such, it was a little higher level of sophistication. If you saw the movie *The Godfather*, directed by Francis Ford Coppola, or if you've read the book by Mario Puzo, this probably best fits in with what Wales must have been like. The gangster knew a new mafia is coming into town and pushing drugs—something the established mob isn't into. As we know, a strategy has be formed on how to stop it, and it had to have a high degree of finesse.

It's not quite the same with the Celtic kings, but the principle is the same. In the Celtic world, the Druids called the shots, and the kings had to listen. It was in very bad form to go against a Druid's decision. No doubt when it was found how Arthur successfully beat off the Saxons attacking Dumonia, he was selected to conduct the northern campaign against the Picts and the Scots. From Nennius's account, Arthur proved his worth. In the 12 great battles over 10 years or more, the Britons were successful. Then news came the Anglo-Saxons were marching up the Thames. It is not surprising Arthur knew how to handle it.

The Battle of Baden lasted for three days. The Britons held tightly onto a very small crest of a steep hill in a locked shield formation, while their cavalry continuously harassed the flanks of the Saxons. The Saxons did not have a cavalry, and so it was an unfair match even though they had superior numbers. The end was a foregone conclusion.

Now that we have the atmosphere and the events, it's time to finish on the real Arthur. The big one is the records. There really isn't a lot on the time, but that's because it's all from one source in a secluded part of the country. However, what there is clearly points out there was an Arthur in the correct time frame, and there's no other around from the other kingdoms. What scholars want from this is an actual book-like document to verify the fact. Nennius is the only one who fulfils this requirement. Going through local records of mundane, everyday activities like land grants hardly interests those in academia. Then there is the standard Celtic bard, which was still in common use in Dark Ages Briton as the official method of recording history. Here, there is an overabundance of evidence of Arthur, such as the famed *Y Goddodin*. Yet not acceptable. ridiculous when you think about it. Ireland, Scotland, Wales and Cornwall today officially accept the bardic interpretation for generic records of royal lineages, but not for historical events. They will accept a King Arthur existed as King of Glamorgan between AD 478 and 536, but not the king of the Britons for the exact same time frame. Bizarre!

On the same note is the books themselves that scholars accept, as well as ones they don't accept. Because Gildus did not mention King Arthur, his book is accepted. However, because Nennius did mention Arthur, his book is not accepted. Bede also did not mention Arthur, so of course his book is accepted. The irony is that all three are continuously used to this very day as references to the existence of Arthur. It's a bit of a contradiction when one thinks about it. One would think if Nennius is not accepted, he would be eliminated from the list. Unfortunately, scholars can't do that because they know the fame of King Arthur was due to Geoffrey of Monmouth, and it turns out he used Nennius as his primary reference. The great academia is caught in an enormous conundrum.

Arthur doesn't exist by way of selective processing, and that's all it is. A king named Arthur did in fact exist in the precise time frame of the legendary Arthur, but because Gildus failed to mention him in absolute terms, the two Arthurs are not the same. Finding the legendary Arthur in these terms is another bizarre set of explanations in which the scholars end up being just as creative as the bards themselves. It's like the fact there was an Arthur who fought at Baden and Camlann, but the fact is we don't know who he was. The question I ask is, Is this possible? A strange man appears out of nowhere, and in a period of 20 years, he magically shows up twice in two confirmed real events. Then as quickly as he shows up, he disappears again. Think about it. If he were a murderer, we know for a fact this mystery wouldn't exist for a moment. The real reason is likely more political than academic.

King Arthur is always examined in the conventional, modern, Western scope. If he were a king like any other king of the Western world, where is his kingdom? Fair enough. However, that way of thinking only applies to the medieval period; before that was Rome, and before that was the Iron Age. Kings as we know them today didn't exist back then. Rome had emperors, and the Celts elected their leaders. There is enough proof of this in the letters of Julius Caesar alone. Unfortunately, we don't think on a broad scale when we examine a single subject; we only think on the specific and nothing else.

The story of Arthur is only going to be accepted as it was told, and as everyone knows it. He lived in Camelot, which can't be found. He had a super sword, which also can't be found. He was married to a beautiful woman, but there is no evidence of her. He fought the Saxons in shining armour that did not exist. He had a nephew whom he killed at Camlann, and there is no evidence of his existence. He is now buried somewhere that no one can find. From the 3 main books that scholars accept on this version of the story, only one mentions the name Arthur. In this light, it is only too easy to dismiss King Arthur as ever having exited.

Unfortunately, the world doesn't work like that when it comes to real facts. They could never prove Al Capone was ever involved in murder, but they did find out he was involved in tax evasion, and so they got him on that. Using the same outside technique, we can prove there was an Arthur, and it is completely believable he is also the same Camelot Arthur.

There was an Arthur who lived in the exact same time frame as the legendary Arthur. The land deeds prove that. This Arthur was a Silures, the most feared warriors in all of Briton, and we have Tacitus to prove that point. We know he was better at fighting than any of his contemporaries. From the official accounts of Tewdrig and Meirig, Arthur came from a long line of intelligent leaders, meaning he was well above his contemporaries when it came to intellect. Ambrosius Aurelianus, often credited as being the real Arthur, is confirmed by numerous sources to be dead by AD 475, so we know he was not around when Badon took place. Government records accept bard lineage accounts for past leaders, and so it would be hypocritical of scholars to not accept them as well. Further to that point is that the official records that Arthur's name is clearly written and sealed; these especially cannot be ignored. Then this leads us to the phenomenon of everything that was written about King Arthur in the 7th century. The legend of Arthur did not start with Geoffrey of Monmouth. As Lady Charlotte Guest proved, it began almost immediately after his death. By the time the 11th century rolled around, there was already a mountain of evidence that Arthur was a real person.

The version we have of King Arthur today, which scholars continue to use as their premise to the true King Arthur, is from a fictional compilation called *Le Morte d'Arthur* by Thomas Malory. It is a fictional story, and using it rather than official government records as a basis for a historical fact exposes a serious lack of common sense.

In my quest to know whether King Arthur was in fact true, my evidence is more inclusive and appears to support the fact the man was a true historical figure.

Bibliography

Anderson, A. O. *Adomnán's Life of Columba*. Oxford: Oxford Press, 1991.

Alcock, L. *The Neighbours of the Picts: Angles and Scots*. London: Roisemarkie, London, 1993.

Ashley, Mike. *King Arthur, The Man and the Legend*. London: Running Press, 2010.

Bain, Ian. *Celtic Knotwork*. London: Constable Publishing, 1986.

Barber, Chris. *King Arthur, The Mystery Unraveled*, Yorkshire, UK: Pen and Sword Books, 2016.

Barnes, Ian. *The Historical Atlas of the Celtic World*. New York: Chartwell Books, Inc., 2010.

Bede the Venerable. *The Ecclesiastical History of the English People*. Script, Northumbria, AD 673.

Blair, John. *The Anglo-Saxon Age*. Oxford: Oxford University, 1984.

Blond, Anthony. *The Private Lives of the Roman Emperors*. London: Running Press, 2008.

The Book of Ulster. Fifth century, monastic.

Breatnach, R. A. (translator). *The Book of Uí Mhaine*. Lecture, Dublin, 1943.

Byrne, E. J. *Niall of the Nine Hostages* (*In Irish Kings and Queens*). London: Oxford, 1973.

Cahill, Thomas. *How the Irish Saved Civilization*. New York: Anchor Books, 1995.

Carver, Martin. *Surviving in Symbols: A Visit to the Pictish Nation*, Edinburgh: Osprey, 1999.

Castleden, Rodney. *King Arthur*. London: Rutledge, 2000.

Chadwick, Nora. *The Celts*. London: The Folio Society, 2002.

———. *The Druids*. Wales: University of Wales, 1997.

Clark, Graham. *Prehistoric England*. London: F. E. Bording, 1940.

Clarkson, Tim. *The Makers of Scotland*. Edinburgh: Birlinn, 1988.

Cumming, W. A. *The Age of the Picts*. London: Suttan Alan, 1995.

Cunliffe, Barry. *The Celts: A Very Short Introduction*. London: Oxford University Press, 2003.

———. *Britain Begins*. London: Oxford University Press, 2012.

Curley, Walter. *Vanishing Kingdoms: The Irish Chiefs and Their Families*. Dublin: Lilliput Press, 2004.

Delaney, Frank. *The Celts*. London: Grafton Books, London, 1986.

De La BeDoyere, Guy. *Roman Britain*. New York: Thames and Hudson, 2006.

Donoghue, C. N. *History of the Celts*. Vancouver: FriesenPress, 2013.

———. *The Irish Empire*. Vancouver: FriesenPress, 2015.

Dudley, Donald. *The Civilization of Rome*. Winnipeg: Meridan Classic, 1962.

Eleure, Christine. *The Celts: The First Masters of Europe*. New York: Abraham, 1993.

Ellis, Peter Berresford. *The Druids*. Michigan: Eerdmans Publishing, 1994.

Fields, Nic. *Rome's Saxon Shore, AD 250–500*. Oxford: Osprey Publishing, 2006.

Foster, Roy (editor). *The Oxford Illustrated History of Ireland*. Oxford: Oxford University Press, 2001.

Foster, Sally. *Picts, Gaels and Scots*. England: B. T. Batsford, 2012.

Gildas the Wise. *De Excidio et Conquestu Britanniae*. Script, Northumbria, AD 570.

Gidlow, Christopher. *The Reign of Arthur*. Gloustershire: Sutton Publishing, 2004.

Goldsworth, Adrian. *The Fall of the West: The Death of the Roman Superpower*. London: Weilfield & Nicolson, 2009.

Grant, Michael. *The Fall of the Roman Empire*. New York: Collier Books, 1976.

Green, Alice S. *History of the Irish State to 1014*. London: Macmillan, 1929.

Griffin, Justin E., *Glastonbury and the Grail*, United Kingdom: McFarland. 2012.

Jackson, K. H. *The Evolution of the Goedelic Language*. British Academy, 1997.

James, Simon. *The World of the Celts*. London: Thames and Hudson, 1993.

Keating, Geoffrey, David Comyn, Patrick S. Dinneen (trans.). *The History of Ireland*. 4 Volumes, 1766.

Konstan, Angus. *Strongholds of the Picts*. London: Osprey, 2010.

Laing, Lloyd and Jenny Laing. *The Picts and the Scots*. Gloucestershire Stroud: Sutton Publishing Ltd, 1994.

Guest, Lady Charlotte. *The Mabinogian*. London: HarperCollins Publishers, 2002.

Lavin, P. *The Celtic World*. New York: Hippocrene Books Inc., 1999.

Livy: The Early History of Rome. Aubrey De Selincourt (trans.). London: Penguin Books, 1960.

Malory, Thomas. *Le Mortre d'Arthur*. Hammonworth (ed.). United Kingdom: Penguin, 1969.

Mallory, Thomas. *Tales of King Arthur*. Michael Senior (ed.). New York: Shocken Books, 1981.

Mallory, J. P. *The Origins of the Irish*. New York: Thames and Hudson, 2013.

Marcellinus, Ammianus. *Res Gestae*. Kimberly Kagan (trans). Connecticut: Yale, 1972.

Mathew, Caitlin. *The Celtic Tradition*. Rockport: Elemental Book Limited, 1995.

Mathews, John. *King Arthur and the Grail Quest*. London: Brochampton Press, 1995.

———. *The Grail: The Truth behind the Myth*. London: Godfrey Books, 2015.

MacAuley, Donald (ed.). *The Celtic Languages*. Cambridge: Cambridge University Press, 2008.

MacKillop, James. *Dictionary of Celtic Mythology*. New York: Oxford University Press, 1998.

McClure, Judith. Bede, *The Ecclesiastical History of the English People*, Oxford: Oxford University, 1969.

Markele, Jean. *The Grail*. Rochester: Inner Tradition, 1999.

———. *The Celtic King*. Rochester: Inner Tradition, 1976.

Meyer, Kuno. *The Death of Niall of the Nine Hostages*. New York: Oxford University Press, 1900.

Molloy, J. P. *The Origins of Ireland*. London: Thames and Hudson, 2010.

Mountford, Paul Rhys, *Ogham, Destiny Books*, Vermont, 2001

Nutt, David for the Irish Texts Society. London 1902–14Kinsella, T., (trans), The Tain.

Ó Cléirigh, Fr. Michael. *The Annals of the Four Masters*. Ireland: Sligo, 1632.

O'Railly, T. F. *Niall of the Nine Hostages*. Dublin: Trinity Press, 1946.

Konstan, Angus. *British Forts in the Age of Arthur.* London: Osprey Books, 2008.

The Strong Holds of the Picts. London: Oxford, 2011.

Piggett, S. *The Druids.* London: Thames and Hudson, 1968.

Plutarch. *Fall of the Roman Republic.* Rex Warner (trans.). Harmondsworth: Penguin Books, 1958.

———. *Makers of Rome.* Ian Scott-Kilvert (trans.). Harmondsworth: Penguin Books, 1965.

———. *The Rise of the Roman Empire.* Ian Scott-Kilvert (trans.). Harmondsworth: Penguin Books, 1979.

Pryor, Francis. *Britain AD.* London: Harper Perennial, 2004.

Radston, Ian. *Celtic Fortification.* Gloucestershire: The Tempus Publishing Ltd, 2006.

Rankin, H. D. *Celts and the Classical World.* London: Croom Helm, 1987.

Richie, Anna. *The Picts.* Edinburgh: Osprey, 1989.

Ridgeway, William. *Niell of the Nine Hostages.* New York: Junior Roman Studies, 1924.

Rodgers, Nigel. *The Roman World: People and Places.* London: Lorenz Books, 2005.

Stirling, Simon Andrew. *The King Arthur Conspiracy.* London: The History Press, 2012.

Sutherland, Elizabeth. *In Search of the Picts.* London: Constable, 1993.

Venning, Timothy. *The Kings and Queens of Wales.* Gloucestershire: Amberley, 2012.

Ward-Perkins, Bryan. *The Fall of Rome.* New York: University of Oxford, 2005.

Weekly, T. H. (translator). *Pictish Chronicles.* Edinborough, AD 971.

Wynford, Thomas V. *A History of Wales.* London: Michael Joseph Ltd, 1985.

Printed in the United States
By Bookmasters